HEALING THROUGH THE SACRAMENTS

Healing Through the Sacraments

Michael Marsch

translated by
Linda M. Maloney

 **THE LITURGICAL PRESS**
Collegeville, Minnesota 56321

Healing Through the Sacraments was originally published by Verlag Styria (Graz and Vienna in Austria and Cologne in West Germany) in 1987 under the title *Heilung durch die Sakramente.*

Cover design by Mary Jo Pauly and Don Bruno.

Printed in the United States of America.

1	2	3	4	5	6	7	8	9

Library of Congress Cataloging-in-Publication Data

Marsch, Michael, 1932–
   [Heilung durch die Sakramente. English]
   Healing through the sacraments / Michael Marsch.
     p. cm.
   Translation of: Heilung durch die Sakramente.
   ISBN 0-8146-1807-3
   1. Sacraments—Catholic Church. 2. Spiritual healing.
3. Catholic Church—Doctrines. I. Title.
BX2203.M38 1989   89-38223
234'.16—dc20   CIP

"Where do you get your inspiration?"
"From Jesus and the sacraments."
—Mother Teresa

Contents

Foreword   9

ONE **Come, Everything Is Prepared:
Invitation to the Feast of the Poor**   11

TWO **Healing Through the Sacrament of the Church**   18

THREE **Healing Through the Sacrament of Baptism**   26

FOUR **Healing Through the Sacrament of Confirmation**   36

FIVE **Healing Through the Eucharist**   44

SIX **Healing Through the Sacrament of Reconciliation**   64

SEVEN **Healing Through the Sacrament of Orders**   79

EIGHT **Healing Through the Sacrament of Marriage**   87

NINE **Healing Through the Sacrament of Anointing**   95

TEN **Healing Through Mary
and the Communion of Saints**   101

Foreword

Human experience is never simply the sum of what has happened to oneself: it rests on the knowledge of generations and centuries. What the Church calls "tradition" is not the sum of individual perceptions and creeds but the handing down of these as a unified whole. More than anything else it is their living presence in the hearts of individuals insofar as they acknowledge themselves part of this whole as, in Paul's expression, members of the body of Christ.

This book is intended to be a report of the experience of God's love to God's people; neither systematic nor exhaustive but simply love experienced and healing perceived—the sense of having been personally touched by what has happened from the days of God's revelation in the Scriptures to our own time. The witnesses of history will have a voice in this story, which at the same time is always the history of salvation: the evangelists, the Church Fathers, and the great saints and teachers of the Church will be heard, but also and especially the Church's statements about itself: the documents of the councils, particularly Vatican Council II (1962–1965).

Some texts in the Church's tradition will sound strange at first and will arouse an instinctive resistance in the reader, primarily because their language and style of thought are unfamiliar. Instincts are certainly good, and criticism of the Church is necessary, but we cannot make the Church a plaything of our wishes and our deficient information about what the Church is, what it intends, and what it teaches. When we do that, we deprive the Church of its ability to heal. We deny ourselves the medicine that alone is able to touch and alter us at our secret depths, where no other agent and no other therapy can reach. We deprive ourselves of that healing that we need most at the present time in order to survive—not only physically.

Sacraments are visible signs of an invisible healing: "medicine for immortality," according to St. Ignatius of Antioch, one of the Church's first bishops. He was speaking of the Eucharist. Celebrating the sacraments means encountering our God and God's love in a very human way. The sacraments are meant to be experienced as personal encounters with Christ in his Church, so that the healing we so urgently need can go forth from them. It is the task of this little book to contribute to that experience.

I wish to thank all those with whom I was able to celebrate the sacraments in recent years and thereby to experience signs and wonders. Because the Word has become flesh, salvation is to be revealed anew, again and again, in the healing of body, mind, and spirit. I have learned most about God's healing power in the continual renewal of the common experience of God's love to the Church—how well God knows each individual and how near God wishes to be to us all.

Pentecost 1986

ONE

Come, Everything Is Prepared: Invitation to the Feast of the Poor

> When one of those who sat at table with him heard this, he said to him, "Blessed is he who shall eat bread in the kingdom of God." But he said to him, "A man once gave a great banquet, and invited many; and at the time for the banquet he sent his servant to say to those who had been invited, "Come; for all is now ready." But they all alike began to make excuses. The first said to him, "I have bought a field, and I must go out and see it; I pray you, have me excused." And another said, "I have bought five yoke of oxen, and I go to examine them; I pray you, have me excused." And another said, "I have married a wife, and therefore I cannot come." So the servant came and reported this to his master. Then the householder in anger said to his servant, "Go out quickly to the streets and lanes of the city, and bring in the poor and maimed and blind and lame . . . that my house may be filled" (Luke 14:15-23).[1]

"Come; for all is now ready," the master of the house has them say. But no one comes—at least, none of those who were invited. And why not? The reasons they politely offer do not seem particularly persuasive: new fields, new oxen, new wives. We would say: new houses, new cars, new partners. . . . It could scarcely be more banal.

Oddly enough, the same excuses that seem so flat here show up elsewhere as legal grounds, not for avoiding a feast

but for refusing military service. In Deut 20:5-7 we find the
same three arguments, almost word for word, but augmented
with a broader one that seems to be the key to the other three:
"What man is there that is fearful and fainthearted? Let him
go back to his house," (Deut 20:8). Cowardice in the face of
the enemy as a legitimate motive for avoiding military service?
Far from it! The text is psychologically subtle. It continues: "lest
the heart of his fellows melt as his heart." Whoever takes up
weapons should be *totally* committed. Halfheartedness is catch-
ing; it undermines the fighting spirit of the troops.

Jesus must have been acquainted with this kind of argu-
ment. What was he thinking of when he quoted it in the parable? What do excuses for staying away from a festival
dinner—the meal in the reign of God, as the text says—have
to do with legal refusal of military service? Since when is a feast
a life and death challenge like a war? And not only for individuals but for a whole people? Is there more at stake in this
meal than eating and drinking? A fundamental decision perhaps? A yes or no to the master of the house? A yes or no to
myself and the other guests?

When Jesus seems to conceal himself in silence, we turn
to the context. At the beginning of chapter 14 in the introduction to the parable of the wedding feast, there is a report of
the healing of a man with dropsy on the Sabbath. The Son of
God is not intent on setting himself above the commandments
of the order of creation (he never does); instead, Jesus feels
it urgent to glorify the Father here and now by reestablishing
the order that was destroyed by this man's fatal illness. None
of the scribes dare to oppose him.

Gift, Not Claim

Then, at the center of chapter 15, we find the parable of
the prodigal son. It acts as a commentary to the parable of the
wedding feast. Here again it is a matter of life and death: "My
son was dead, and is alive again; he was lost, and is found."
So the father answers the embittered question of the older

son—why the father has prepared a boisterous feast for the younger son who has wasted his whole inheritance in foreign parts, while the older son, who has always lived and worked by his father's side, has never received even a word of recognition for it. And what is the father's answer? "Everything that I have is yours, my son." *Everything*—but the son never knew how to accept, recognize, or value any of it. He thought his wages had to be paid him to the exact nickel and penny. He thought he had a right to recompense for his services. He could not see the unearned gift of living in the father's presence— just as the younger son had been unable to see the undeserved gift that was his inheritance from the father. He had also thought he had a legal right to it. Both sons are equally lost. Both of them are among the rich, because they think they have a *claim* to something the father wants to offer them as undeserved *gift*. But this very gift of the father is what neither of them can see.

Apparently, riches make people blind, and not only blind but lame as well. The older brother does not want to go to the feast for the younger. "He was angry and refused to go in"— just like the invited guests in the parable of the wedding feast in chapter 14. They too find the invitation more of a burden or compulsion than a joy and an honor. And so the master of the house invites other guests—this time from the streets: the poor, the lame, the crippled, and the blind. There is not a word to say why he so suddenly changes his mind. Here also the context must come to our aid.

Jesus tells the parable of the invitation to the wedding feast at a time when he himself is the dinner guest of a Pharisee—a celebrity on a par with other prominent people. And as prologue to the parable, he first explains to his host just whom one ought to invite to dinner and whom one should not invite: *not* those who can return the invitation—the well-off and the well-meaning, the respectable types and those who like to be seen. Instead, one should invite those who cannot return the favor, those whom nobody wants and nobody would approach: the poor, the lame, the crippled, and the blind. If

Jesus has to say that so pointedly, we may conclude that even the scribes, who were so anxious to appear as models in all things, did not always adhere to this traditional precept.[2]

And why not? Because the poor, the lame, the crippled, and the blind are people who disturb a banquet: in the first place through their appearance, their behavior, their way of speaking and expressing themselves; but also because in their presence one is no longer "among friends," among those who belong and know that they do, who extend invitations in order to receive them, who see one another in order to be seen, who affirm one another in order to be affirmed. The poor and lame, the crippled and blind, however, don't belong anywhere. Nobody wants them, nobody wants to see them. They are unwelcome, annoying, excluded. They are different from the others—and people let them know that they are different and will stay that way. We let them feel that they are disturbing.

Our Own Poverty Revealed

And why are they so upsetting? Why are they unwanted? The answer is simple: because they raise questions. Everything and everybody is called into question nowadays. It is a matter of good form not to leave anything as it is and not to believe anything as it stands. But the poor, by their very *existence*, reveal things within *me* that ought not to be questioned: their awkwardness turns a spotlight on my own helplessness, their isolation uncovers my own insecurity, their wandering condition makes my own homelessness obvious. In the depth of my heart I am no less poor, no less handicapped, than those I call "the poor" and "the handicapped"—and to whom I prefer to give a wide berth. I don't want to acknowledge that I am like "them" and so I acquire new fields, new oxen, new spouses, new houses, new cars, new partners. . . . But it is precisely in my dependence on constantly renewed wealth that my poverty reveals itself more and more clearly. My handicap shows itself in everything that prevents me from accepting the invitation. The more I have, the more plans I have. I have everything—except time. I can't very well say: "I am an important person," but I can always say: "*Unfortunately* I haven't time"—and it comes to pretty much the same thing. My appointment calendar is full. All the possible dates are taken. There just isn't time for anything more.

But if riches are so desirable and if it is characteristic of all who have them that they have no time, why did God become human among the poorest and why did Jesus have so much time for *them* above all? Why was it that he was born between two animals and died between two terrorists—and why was he so attracted to tax collectors and whores? And why are the signs he left behind after his earthly life so pitifully poor? Why should it be bread and wine? And why did he have to wash his disciples' feet? Why not something spectacular?

I had to endure a Holy Thursday service in which the foot washing before the Last Supper was replaced by a color slide. That is a scandal, a real offense! Why do we try to deny the simplicity of the signs? Why must our worship services be so elaborate? Are we perhaps afraid of the essential? Are we embarrassed when the priest washes people's naked feet before the altar? Does it cut too close? Get under our skin? Are we frightened in face of the poverty of our God? Is this feast really about life and death? Did he really not come to bring peace, but a sword? To cast fire on the earth, desiring that it be kindled?

I also had to sit through a service in which the Scripture readings were replaced by a text from Kafka. That is another scandal! The Lord of the Church forbidden to speak in his own house? The Word of the incarnate God too paltry? Too flat in its sobriety? Its love too penetrating? Was Augustine right when he said: "The word of God is your enemy"? What else did this great saint and teacher have to say? "The word of God is your enemy. It is the adversary of your will until it becomes the author of your salvation. . . . As long as you are your own enemy, the Word of God remains your enemy as well. Become your own friend and you will live in harmony with the Word."[3]

So is it really war? In the middle of the feast? A life and

death struggle? "Lord, my servant is dying—but only say the word . . . ."? War with the Word made flesh? War with the Word that invites me to the wedding feast? War with the Word that gives itself as my food? But why this continual war? Why can't this festive meal be a gentler thing? Why can't Jesus find more appropriate words, more aesthetic gestures?

Self-Importance, a Shield Against Self-Knowledge

Or are the slide of the foot washing and the text from Kafka intended to protect me from the eventuality that this war, which has been building up in *me* for a long time, could break out in the middle of the feast? That *my* war could burst forth like a thunderstorm, a colossal flood that uproots and over-whelms everything? But where is this war in me? Whom should I hate and wish to destroy, at best to chop in little pieces? I have never had anything *against* the poor and lame! I am happy for them that they fill the hall after the rich have all sent their excuses. Or, if I look more closely, will it turn out that those are *my* poor and lame who are shoving their way forward, *my* blindness and crippling that are preferred by the Lord of the house?

Down with the ages-long oppression by the rich? Down with all the new fields, oxen, spouses? Down with the new houses, cars, partners? Down with the whole wealth of my functions: with the church trustee, parish council chair, prayer group leader in me? Put an end to my whole career of church activism—just because the Lord of the house prefers the poor and lame?

What does Augustine say? "Be your own friend, and you will live in harmony with the Lord's word." In other words, acknowledge your poverty, admit your lameness, confess that you are blind and crippled before the Lord—and the feast of the Word will no longer be a war for you, but instead the "au-thor of your salvation." You won't have to look for slides of the foot washing or Kafka texts in the Liturgy of the Word. You will no longer let yourself be betrayed by the president of the liturgy committee in your heart. You no longer need to hide your poverty beneath what you think are riches. You need never again excuse yourself from the wedding feast because of your new oxen. At last, you can join the feast as one of the poor and lame, the crippled and blind, whom the Lord of the house loves so much.

Notes

1. Scripture quotations are from the Revised Standard Version of the Bible, copyrighted 1946, 1952, © 1971, 1973 by the Division of Christian Education of the National Council of the Churches of Christ in the U.S.A., and are used by permission. Some quotations, marked with an asterisk (*), have been slightly adapted in harmony with the author's German or to provide more inclusive expression.

2. E.g., Lev 25:35.

3. *Enarrationes in Psalmos* 129:3.

TWO

Healing Through the Sacrament of the Church

I once asked a psychotherapist friend of mine how he could explain the fact that horrifying visions of shocking brutality seem to appear and reappear so often in young people's dreams: living persons are ground up, carried along conveyer belts to be thrown into a huge pit, stirred by irradiated robots, and yet are still alive, staring at the dreamer, opening their mouths in silent screams. . . . "We see and hear too much," was the answer. "We experience more than we can cope with."

In this conversation we were talking mainly about Hiroshima and Chernobyl. But whether it is a question of the Holocaust, of Turks in the mines, of hunger in India, of genetic manipulations on the television screen or embryos in retort glasses, in all cases we not only want to see what is happening "at the bottom" of the mines but also "at the bottom" of ourselves.[1] Our pleasure in destruction seems to be endless. We go on with business as usual, as if nothing had happened. Of course, after the fact everything is criticized, investigated, picked to pieces. But one gets used to that, too.

What do I think about, after all, if I have a headache? Aspirin. And what do I think of if it gets worse? The doctor. What will the doctor do? Ask questions, make tests, write a prescription. Maybe she or he will have a consoling word for me. That will help. But what else? What is the result? How much more do I know than I did before, as I go on with my referral to the next doctor? Don't I leave in a state of greater uncertainty than when I came? At least the man or woman in the white coat should have known. . . . She or he *had* to know what was wrong with me.

What good to me is the best diagnosis if I no longer know myself? What do I mean when I say, "I am ill"? What am I looking for when I seek "healing"? Don't I expect something from the doctors that they really *cannot* give? Isn't the thing I am looking for beyond their capacity? beyond what they *must* and *may* know? Doctors are there to relieve symptoms. That is their greatness and their limitation.[2]

The Underlying Need to Belong

But in that case, why did I go to the doctor at all? Didn't I know beforehand that it wouldn't help much? That the doctor would say that my loss of hearing would go away—and that she or he was not competent in the matter of mothers-in-law? So what am I looking for? Maybe the doctor of souls to whom I can finally unburden myself? And yet, without my knowing it, my longing reaches still further: the child in me longs for its father, for its mother. And what a grownup does not dare to say out loud, the body screams, in headaches and loss of hearing—the voice of the child that refuses to go on playing the game.

Here already, illness reveals itself as a quite different kind of reality, and healing as a much more comprehensive expectation than the one I would care to admit to myself. What I am looking for is not so much relief of my symptoms; rather, it is the security of *belonging*—a little bit of intact world. I want someone to hold my hand, stroke my head, embrace me as a mother does. . . .

All that and much more the Church—yes, the Church, of all things—wants to offer me, when it says of itself in a language that is not always accessible at first reading: "By her relationship with Christ, the Church is a kind of sacrament of intimate union with God, and of the unity of all [hu]mankind. . . ."[3] Still—the Church here offers itself to us as a possibility for "intimate union with God and . . . the unity of all humankind." But how does it propose to communicate to me that sense of *security of belonging* that I want more desperately than anything else?

If I read the New Testament stories of healing with this question in my heart, my *first* impression is that Jesus heals in a much more modern fashion than today's Church: he gives precise and definite cures for precise and definite requests. Someone is blind and wants to see, and Jesus restores his sight to him. Someone is lame and wants to walk, and Jesus says: "Stand up, take your bed and go!"

When we read the healing stories in this way, of course, we do not notice that this kind of reading is a projection. We read into the text of the Bible what *we today* understand healing to be: the relief of symptoms. But Jesus wants to do infinitely more than simply to alleviate our pain and deliver us from handicaps. What is the healing that *he* offers us?

If we turn to the early Church Fathers, those who are closest in time to the evangelists, for their testimony of the way *they* understand Jesus' healing, we get a very different picture from the one that *we* find in the New Testament reports in response to our own expectations and ideas. At first glance, the early Church Fathers' understanding of Jesus' cures seems to us very disappointing. In their commentaries on encounters between Jesus and sick people there is at first not even a mention of the relief of symptoms. If we look more closely, we discover that for them the simple disappearance of symptoms seems much too superficial to warrant their spending time on a discussion of something so obvious. What *they* find interesting are those *invisible* realities that Jesus wants to make clear to us through visible signs (whose actuality the Fathers do not doubt).

Healing Understood as Unity

More precisely, the early Church Fathers want to know what *symbolic* value Jesus' healings have for the people. Of course, at this point we have to be clear about the meaning of the word "symbolic." The Greek word *symbolon* describes the two halves of a broken coin, ring, or staff. "Symbolic" means seeing the unity of different aspects of a single reality— in the case of Jesus' healings, being able to see *simultaneously* the visible, physically recognizable event *and* its visible spiritual reality. To recognize clearly the unity of both aspects of the one reality is especially important today. For on the one hand the Church has preached for centuries that the stories about Jesus' cures were to be understood in an exclusively spiritual sense: Jesus wanted to open for the blind "the eyes of the heart." To think of a physical change would be much too banal. And on the other hand many people today are in danger of going to the opposite extreme, namely, believing exclusively in physical healing while forgetting what dimensions of the inbreaking reign of God are supposed to be revealed in the fact that a blind person recovers his or her eyesight. The early Church Fathers' understanding of Jesus' healings is so important in giving direction to our own thinking because in their eyes Jesus did not tell stories that anyone can reinterpret at will; instead, as human and divine being, he makes a history that is always and at every moment salvation history as well.

The healing stories in the New Testament often served the early Church as a basis for catechetical instruction about the Easter mysteries of the suffering, death, and resurrection of Jesus. Apparently, the first Christians already had a problem in comprehending the breadth, height, and depth of these events. So they needed examples that would illuminate the events or at least lead people into the mystery. In fact, it is not difficult to detect a section on suffering, death, and resurrection in the arrangement of many of the healing stories told by the four evangelists. Therefore we may easily conclude that the redactors of the Gospels had a catechetical purpose in mind when composing the healing stories. They used illustrations in an effort to ease the readers' approach to the Easter event.[4] But this also shows that the first Christians had an incomparably broader idea of sickness and healing than we have today. For Jesus, *the* "source of illness" was quite obviously original sin—that which separated humanity from the divine order of creation, the source of all life and health.[5]

Through disobedience and self-glorification, the human being was in danger of separation from the divine order of creation. But that would lead not only to destruction of that order and thereby to the mortality of the human creature but especially and primarily to the limitation of human life on earth. Created in the image of God, the human being was originally designed, like God, for everlasting life. It was through disobedience, that is, separation from God as the source of life, that people themselves set limits on their earthly life (cf. Gen 3:23).

Belonging Restored in the Body of Christ

If "sickness," then, refers to human mortality and the limitation of human life through separation from God's wholeness, "healing"[6] in the first place means nothing other than the saving of human beings from this limitation through the gift of everlasting life. Only after that, as an added gift, does healing also mean rescue from mortality, or to put it in modern terms, from symptoms.

But still more: Jesus not only became human in order to free human beings from the yoke of disobedience (that is, from the limitedness of our life) through his loving obedience even to death on a cross; Jesus was also bodily raised from the dead so that we may have everlasting life in him and may be raised bodily with him. This grace is not something we will receive only after our bodily death, but it is ours already in *this* life, through the sacrament of baptism in which we enter here and now into his death and resurrection: "You are no longer strangers and sojourners, but you are fellow citizens with the saints and members of the household of God," as the apostle

Paul says about the effects of our baptism (Eph 2:19). The "saints" in the New Testament are all those who have been hallowed by entering into Jesus' death and resurrection—all the baptized as members of his mystical body, the Church.

If we come to understand sickness and healing as realities of such dimensions, it may become somewhat clearer to us why, for the early Church, it was not only the physician but more especially the Church that was responsible for healing—and why even today it is only the Church that is able to take hold of every kind of illness at its unique, deepest, and toughest root, namely, sin. Through separation from God as source of life and wholeness, sin causes not only illness but death. Behind it is the one whom John calls "a murderer from the beginning" and "the father of lies" (John 8:44).

It is he, finally, who is behind the human desire for self-destruction. There is only *one* power that can withstand him, namely the Church as the *body of Christ*, the One who, by his death, overcame death. And this power is, in particular, the Church as the sacrament that it is, for this alone is able to heal us by leading us back to the *sources* of wholeness: "The Church is a kind of sacrament of intimate union with God, and of the unity of all [hu]mankind."[7]

The Church as the "fundamental sacrament" is revealed to us in the most effective and concrete way in those signs of God's love that we call the sacraments. The sacraments are not intended to fool us with fantasies about a sound and integral world. They are neither drugs nor magic. Jesus did not promise us a rose garden. But through a personal encounter with the Savior in his Church, the sacraments can make a decisive contribution toward the healing of individuals in a less and less whole and wholesome world. Individuals will be enabled to find that sense of belonging in the human community that is so seriously lacking today. They will be able to let themselves be healed by the love of God and through a new experience of the bonds of community with sisters and brothers. The following pages will try to show how that can be realized in practice.

Notes

1. Translator's note: The author's reference is to Günter Wallraff's book, *Ganz Unten* (Cologne: Kiepenhauer & Witsch, 1985), a shocking exposé of the treatment of Turkish guest workers in West Germany.

2. A friend of mine suffered quite regularly, after each of his none-too-frequent visits to his mother-in-law, a spell of deafness: he couldn't understand anything. Since his hearing is decisively important for his work, he went to a well-known specialist. He was told that not much could be done; probably it would go away by itself. Luckily, it did. After the third episode, my friend cautiously asked whether there might be some connection between visiting his mother-in-law and losing his hearing. The specialist's answer: "There's no such thing." Because nothing *can* be that *may not* be?

3. Vatican Council II, Dogmatic Constitution on the Church *(Lumen Gentium,* hereafter abbreviated *LG).* Citations are from Walter M. Abbott, S.J., ed., *The Documents of Vatican II* (New York: America Press, 1966).

4. On this subject see my book: *Heilen. Biblische Grundlagen des Heilungsauftrags der Kirche* (Salzburg, 1983), pp. 14–28.

5. Daily contact with sick people shows me more and more clearly that original sin is by no means so old fashioned and abstract a concept as some theologians and their students think nowadays. I ask myself why God became human and "was obedient even to death on a cross" if there never had been such a thing as human disobedience, that is, original sin, and if there were no such thing today.

In plain terms, that means that every form of illness is a consequence of original sin and for that very reason has to be combated decisively and with every means at our disposal. But it does *not* mean, as some think, that every illness is also the result of some particular, personal sin. That *can* be so, as in the case of the lame man (Mark 2:1-12), where bodily lameness is only the outward expression of spiritual crippling. But it *need* not be so, as we see in the healing of a blind man (John 9:1-7), which is only so that "the works of God might be made manifest in him" (v. 3). What really "bothers" us about the reality of original sin is the truth that we cannot save ourselves, that we are dependent on the mercy of another.

6. Translator's note: The author's presentation often depends on a connection between "wholeness" and "holiness" that has been obscured by the development of those words in English but is still clear in the German words "heil," "heilung," "heil," "heilig," and their derivatives. The reader should keep in mind that English "whole" and "holy" stem from the same word and are ultimately identical with German "heil." The word "health," in fact, comes from the same German root.

7. *LG* 1.

THREE

Healing Through the Sacrament of Baptism

"The police dogs' bites don't hurt less—but we can pray for the police officers." That is how Martin Luther King, Jr. explained the effects of baptism and faith in Jesus Christ. It is probably against this background as well that we should understand his saying: "Do whatever you will—we will always love you." Why are such statements not to be counted as masochism? Why are they the opposite of the desire for self-destruction? Why can they only have a healing effect—for the persecutors as well as for the persecuted? Why are they a triumph over evil, even if they lead to death, as they did for Martin Luther King?

Someone could say that in the sacrament of baptism—that is, by our entry into the suffering, death, and resurrection of Jesus—we have already undergone every possible form of persecution, torture, and even martyrdom: *nothing* can separate us from the love of Christ. Such a statement means to say that the police dogs' bites don't hurt less and the assassins' bullets are not less deadly, but that the destruction has lost its *meaninglessness.*

Baptism is a victory of light over the powers of darkness. It lifts human beings up and ends their separation from God. It delivers them from their disobedience, their arrogance, and thus also from their condition as lost and lacking in a sense of belonging. It heals their deepest wounds: those of inner

homelessness and fatherlessness. It fulfills their deepest longing and leads them back to a loving kind of dependence: to
the freedom of the children of God.

If healing, considered biblically, not only means the relief
of symptoms but primarily the elimination of the limitedness
of earthly life through salvation to everlasting life, baptism reveals itself in more than one sense as a sacrament of healing.
In the first place, baptism frees us from original sin through
our entry into the death of Jesus. By our entry into his resurrection it gives us new life: "so that as Christ was raised from
the dead by the glory of the Father, we too might walk in newness of life" (Rom 6:4).

But still more: since through baptism we have been raised
with Christ from the dead—here and now, already in *this* life—
we become members of the mystical *body* of Christ. We are no
longer isolated. We are freed from the sphere of divisions and
tensions, confusion and destruction. "We know that we are
of God, and the whole world is in the power of the evil one,"
as John writes (1 John 5:19). But if we are of God, we are no
longer alone: "you are no longer strangers and sojourners, but
you are fellow citizens with the saints and members of the
household of God" (Eph 2:19).

Thus, our healing through baptism consists of a call to holiness. And this call is not only promise but is already fulfilled.
The "saints" in the Acts of the Apostles and in Paul's letters
are, as we have said, all the baptized, all those who, by entering into Jesus' death and resurrection, have already been sanctified. It is not through our own efforts that we become saints
but through the outpouring of the Holy Spirit on all flesh. But
that indicates a form of healing and thus also a certainty of salvation that can in no way be canceled out: neither by the bites
of the police dogs nor the murderers' bullets nor the internal
murder of sin nor those forms of fear and despair, of destruction and confusion, that can result from it. "You did not receive the spirit of slavery to fall back into fear, but you have
received the spirit of sonship, the Spirit in whom we call:
'Abba, Father' " (Rom 8:15*).

Baptism: A Call to Radical Poverty

That is not to say that baptismal healing guarantees a life without external difficulties and inner suffering. On the contrary, trials of all sorts are to be expected along a way that is to lead us ever closer to Christ. For the gracious gifts of baptism—precisely this way of becoming more and more like Christ—to be able to reshape our lives from the ground up, day by day, there is the need on our part for a radical poverty in the sense of renunciation of those things we have "appropriated" for ourselves: *our* notions of who we are and *our* plans for what we should become. We have to unlearn the business of taking control of our lives and realizing our own self-development. "We leave it to the goodness of God to make plans for the future. For yesterday is past, and tomorrow is not yet here; and we have at our disposal only today in which to recognize Him, to love Him and to serve Him," as it says in the constitution of Mother Teresa's Sisters of Charity.

The parable of the rich young man is a good example of what *not* to do. It is possible to know one's religion very well, to understand it deeply, to follow the commandments faithfully—but all that is worthless. The riches we must surrender do not in any sense have to be the material kind. Material goods may be the easiest to give up. It becomes more difficult when we have to free ourselves of habits of which we may be largely unaware: of a drive for power that is as blind as it is tenacious, from competitive ideals, and from chasing after the favor of those in power (in other words, from "upward mobility"). We can put as pious a face on all this as we want to; we can confuse it with "obedience," or "willingness to serve," but in the end it remains a striving for our own glory.

Why did the rich young man "go away sorrowful," that is, go his own way? Only because he had "great possessions" which he did not want to give up? After all, he was not supposed to simply throw them away, but to give them to the poor in order to store up treasure for himself in heaven and *to follow Jesus*. But it was just this motivation that he seems not to have taken note of. It is not a question of renunciation as a "pious practice"; instead it is an *offer* to make one's way in company with Jesus *easier* by shedding the things that encumber us on the way.

Healing through baptism does not mean taking on some kind of difficult exercises or even tricks for their own sake—that would be no sacrifice; it would be the kind of arrogance from which baptism is supposed to deliver us. Healing through baptism means a closeness to Jesus as the Savior in which nothing happens that is not motivated by love for him.

This is why St. Ignatius of Antioch, a first-century Church Father, in the face of death (he was condemned by the Romans to be thrown to the wild beasts in the arena) was able to implore his brother and sister Christians not to hold him back even if he should weaken:

> I plead with you, do not do me an unseasonable kindness. Let me be fodder for wild beasts—that is how I can get to God. I am God's wheat and I am being ground by the teeth of wild beasts to make a pure loaf for Christ . . . if I suffer, I shall be emancipated by Jesus Christ; and united to him, I shall rise to freedom. . . . That is whom I am looking for—the One who died for us. That is whom I want—the One who rose for us. I am going through the pangs of being born [to new life]. . . . My Desire has been crucified and there burns in me no passion for material things. There is living water in me, which speaks and says inside me, "Come to the Father."[1]

Is this masochism? Quite the contrary: what could appear in someone else as a pure desire for self-destruction becomes in Ignatius a shining witness to Christian faith, that is, an affirmation of life. This "living water" is for him nothing other than the voice of the Holy Spirit, who helps us to call out with childlike trust: "Abba, Father!" In his deep inner union with the suffering and death of Christ as well as with his resurrection, Ignatius longs for that life that is already promised us in baptism, namely, everlasting life. "We are . . . heirs of God and fellow heirs with Christ, provided we suffer with him in order that we may also be glorified with him" (Rom 8:16-17).

So baptism can certainly lead even to martyrdom; in fact, this testimony in blood can be regarded as the most complete fulfillment of our assimilation to Jesus' death on the cross—but also to his resurrection. And thus baptism can bring us to that salvation and healing that we call participation in the glory of God. Ultimately, every one of us is called to be glorified with Jesus.

Of course, this call need not lead to martyrdom for everyone. The life of the baptized has many dimensions. Others among the early Church Fathers saw foreshadowings of baptism in many stages of the history of the people of Israel. An insight into their view of these signs can help us to envision more concretely the various dimensions of baptized life—and so can help us to understand also our tendency to avoid a conscious acceptance of the consequences of our baptism and to deprive ourselves of its healing effects.

Salvation Only Through Interdependence

For example, the passage through the Red Sea was seen by the Church Fathers as a *typos*, a type or image of baptism. They emphasize the rescue of the people in a way that human beings could not even imagine: first the people had to recognize the impossibility of freeing themselves from their situation by their own efforts, and that situation had to appear completely hopeless in their own eyes before God could intervene in order to demonstrate that for *God's* love nothing is impossible. It seems that for us to accept and take seriously God's way of solving problems, all our own attempts at solution must first prove themselves entirely hopeless. Nothing makes us so insecure as securities that we have fashioned for ourselves. The security with which the Jewish people walked dry-shod through the Red Sea could not have been conceived or realized by any human being. But it seemed to be the only *real* solution, namely the salvation of the people and of its individual members by means of protection from a destruction that already appeared inevitable. It was more than healing; it was rescue from certain death, from radical destruction by the enemy. And that is what baptism is and continues to be: we only have to think of it, for example when, in a dangerous situation, we deliberately make the Sign of the Cross and thus unmask the false securities with which we have tried to protect ourselves.

In Israel's forty years of wandering in the desert, the Church Fathers saw the gradual preparation of the people for taking possession of the land. At the beginning, in Miriam's song of thanksgiving for the miraculous passage through the Red Sea (Exod 15), we find mentioned that God has chosen Mount Sion as God's dwelling on earth and that all people will come together there. In a Jewish commentary on the passage we find that all who reject Egyptian slavery accept the yoke of the Torah, but those who put on the yoke of the Torah are freed from the yoke of this world. That is exactly what happens in baptism. We die to the compulsions of sin: in accepting the law of love, we are freed from the rules imposed by life in the world. Because love bears *everything* and endures *everything*, and does so freely, it is love alone that can heal us of the countless "you musts" of every day (most of which we have imposed on ourselves): You must be bigger, better, stronger, more competent than the others. . . . But baptism brings us into a realm where being together means more than doing things for one another.

Being with each other is not an arbitrary action, so that each can live wherever she or he wants to—and then demand of others a tolerance for his or her behavior that can very easily be oppressive. For a demand for tolerance can quickly become a subtle form of pressure: "I will leave you alone if you leave me alone." It can even more easily become a source of discord and disunity and thus also of mischief: each one decides for him- or herself what is right—and the others have to go along with it; they have to "tolerate" me and my behavior. But in its journey through the desert, the people of Israel had to follow if it wanted to stay healthy and move on or even to survive: when the cloud arose, the people had to break

camp; when the cloud descended, they had to stop and en-
camp again. Disobedience through separation from the people
meant certain death for individuals, and at the same time a
weakening of the nation as a whole. One can search the Bible
in vain for a discussion about the cloud's style of leadership.
Such a debate would certainly have led to division, which
would have meant the death of all those involved. No one
would have had the strength to sustain the desert journey
alone; no one would have reached the Promised Land. We cannot hope to meet God and see God's glory alone, but only as
part of God's people, as members of Christ's body.

Dependence, Not Independence

The Church Fathers found another image of baptism in
Moses' drawing water from a rock by striking it with his staff.
In Moses' staff they saw the cross of Christ, in the rock his
dead body from which came forth streams of life-giving water.
Here again we find the idea of the abolition of the limitations
of earthly life through salvation and healing—to everlasting life
in a completely unimaginable and unpredictable way. How
senseless it must have seemed to try to save the people from
certain death of thirst by striking a rock with a staff, expecting
enough water to come forth to slake the thirst of all Israel. But
it is just this faithful obedience of Moses, this spontaneous sacrifice of his independence, that results in the rescue of the
whole nation. Through obedience and the sacrifice of one individual for the salvation of the many, Moses' deed becomes
an image of Jesus and of our baptism in his name.

Something similar can be said of Moses' prayer for the gift
of manna. Without this bread from heaven the people would
have starved; they had reached the limits of earthly survival
and saw no possibility to pass those limits by their own efforts.
But the people are not supposed to gather manna for more than
one day's need, so that they may learn again every day to trust
in God's saving goodness. And what do the people do? They

gather enough to supply them for eight days, in order to make themselves independent—and the manna goes bad.

Certainly, people need institutions and organizations in order to live together—even in the reign of God. But when we try to use these things to become independent of God's merciful love by turning God's gifts into hoarded possessions, these gifts will simply go sour: they can no longer bear fruit, or they will bring forth only rotten fruit. For we are then not even living in God's reign any more but in a self-made world, a world that is necessarily full of unwholesomeness because it is cut off from the source of wholeness, even if its vocabulary seems very holy indeed.

Finally, the Fathers saw another image of baptism in Israel's passage through the Jordan over the "bridge" of twelve stones, as they entered into the Promised Land. In the twelve stones, the Fathers saw prefigured the twelve prophets, the twelve apostles, and the twelve gates of the heavenly Jerusalem. All of them make possible the "passing over" (Pesach) from a temporally limited human life into everlasting life in God's glory.

In the fact that the people had to march seven times around the city of Jericho and praise God with trumpet blasts until the walls fell and the city could be taken captive (as pledge for the capture of the whole land), the Church Fathers saw not only baptism but all seven sacraments as opportunities for the "festive" entry into God's land and thus as access to Mount Sion, to the Temple where God lives among human beings, and to the holy of holies: to God's living presence in our midst. This presence of God heals us and makes us holy by freeing us from all the compulsions and limitations of human life.

Ephata: Be Thou Opened

I was in Jakarta in July of 1983 and saw how the sacrament of baptism can heal and save the life of an adult person even in a borderline situation. Late one evening I was called to the bedside of a Chinese woman. I was told that she had been in a coma since noon. And in fact, I found her lying motionless with her eyes closed, surrounded by at least a dozen relatives who were evidently trying to revive her by rhythmically jogging her limbs. To my astonishment, her husband asked me quietly if I would baptize her. When I objected that in the case of an adult an express personal decision was required for baptism, he replied that she had already been going regularly to church and wanted to be baptized; besides, it was urgent, since the doctors apparently did not know anything else to do for her. I prayed about the matter, and came to the conclusion that it would really be right to baptize her. Since it was July 26, we decided to give her the baptismal name Anna Maria. While I was baptizing her, I remembered that Michael Scanlan and Ann T. Shields, in their book *Their Eyes Were Opened,*[2] reported that Scanlan's two-year-old niece had been healed of deafness by the *ephata* rite at baptism. This ritual, which is frequently omitted nowadays because we are no longer aware of its deep meaning, is intended not only to open the five senses metaphysically for God and God's glory but also to strengthen and heal them physically. Therefore at the baptism of this Chinese woman I prayed the *ephata* ritual very slowly and intensely. As I touched her closed eyelids and said: ''Ephata, be opened!'' she immediately opened her eyes and stared at me. Since I thought we had no common language and I did not know her Chinese name, I could only address her with her new baptismal name, which she could not know. Nevertheless, a contact was established, a dialogue of the eyes. A few hours later she recovered her ability to speak. Four weeks afterward I saw her again. I discovered that she spoke fluent English and I was able to talk with her at length. I became convinced that she had consciously experienced her baptism while in the coma. After a total physical and psychic collapse, a nearly complete cure had taken place through the grace of the sacrament of baptism, and not only a spiritual cure but also a healing of body and mind. She had largely recovered her bodily strength and her mental balance, and still more, she was now beginning a new life as a follower of Christ.

I have never experienced more clearly how much Jesus

desires to heal and sanctify us through baptism, not only in a spiritual sense but by giving us a share in his physical death and bodily resurrection, "so that as Christ was raised from the dead by the glory of the Father, we too might walk in newness of life" (Rom 6:5).

Notes

1. Ignatius to the Romans, 4–8. The text may be found in Cyril C. Richardson, ed., *Early Christian Fathers* (New York: Macmillan/Collier, 1970).

2. Michael Scanlan and Ann Thérèse Shields, *Their Eyes Were Opened: Encountering Jesus in the Sacraments* (Ann Arbor: Word of Life, 1976).

FOUR

Healing Through the Sacrament of Confirmation

"The Holy Spirit gives the fire, and the good works begin," said the Curé of Ars. Because of the gifts of the Holy Spirit, confirmation is a sacrament of healing from two of the deadly sicknesses in the life of a Christian: stress and routine. While it is fashionable today to be overworked, to be "unable to do another thing," it is almost more up to date to suffer from the sheer routine of so much work or, to put it even more bluntly, from boredom. Stress and boredom are, basically, unconscious forms of resignation. They express a kind of creeping hopelessness: "I always have to do everything myself." But that in itself is not realism but illusion—not to mention concealed pride. "How easy are the cares of this world if one has the Holy Spirit," said the Curé of Ars, who was well known as one who was not exactly idle; he got up at one o'clock in the morning and heard confessions for sixteen hours a day. Somewhere else he says: "There are people who find religion boring. That is a sign that they do not have the Holy Spirit." But stress and routine are not only signs of resignation; they also lead inevitably to frustration and a habit of criticizing, and to the most varied forms of aggressiveness. They are both crippling and demoralizing; they are the death of all creativity and community; they lead to marginalization and alienation: to the borders of society and beyond.

36

The sacrament of confirmation is, with baptism and the Eucharist, one of the "sacraments of initiation": it is aimed at *introducing* us more powerfully into the community of human persons with God and into human society—into relationship, love, and service. Everything that is infirm because of the weaknesses of nature should be made firm, confirmed by the gifts of the Spirit. God expects no more from us than we are in a position to give. It is *our* problem that we think we have to manage everything by ourselves. There is no question of that with God: why did God become human? Why did God give us the divine Spirit? So as to leave us to our own fate? The Curé of Ars' phrase: "How easy are the cares of this world if we have the Holy Spirit," seems to be a good yardstick: the degree to which we groan under the burdens of daily labor shows us how little we are allowing the Holy Spirit to supply us with wings for our work, and that also usually indicates how sluggish and monotonous the results will appear.

A Royal Priesthood, a Holy People

Vatican Council II emphasizes no less clearly our radical dependence on the Holy Spirit and on the gifts of the Spirit when it says: ". . . strengthened by the power of the Holy Spirit through confirmation, [we] are assigned to the apostolate by the Lord himself."[1] Thus, confirmation is a strengthening for prophetic service in daily life. This does not refer to the "shining gift" of prophecy, of which the Council speaks elsewhere, but the simple and often hidden witness of the Christian in day-to-day service. The Constitution on the Liturgy says it even more simply: ". . . the liturgy of the sacraments and sacramentals sanctifies almost every event in [our] lives."[2] In other words, it is not *what* we do that is decisive but *how* it takes place, more precisely, how we are present for others. All too often "doing for one another" is nothing but a flight from "being with one another." But it is just this flight into activity that gets in the way of the support and aid of the Holy Spirit, which is offered us in a special way in the sacrament of confirmation.

In connection with confirmation, Vatican Council II speaks of a consecration of laypeople: "They are consecrated [in confirmation] into a royal priesthood and a holy people (cf. 1 Pet 2:4-10) in order that they may offer spiritual sacrifices through everything they do, and may witness to Christ throughout the world. For their part, the sacraments . . . communicate and nourish that charity which is the soul of the entire apostolate."[3] The works of Christians thus have no value in themselves; they acquire value to the extent that they are brought as sacrifices in order to give witness to Christ. To put it in the words of Mother Teresa: "Without faith in Christ there is no love—and without love there is no service of the poor."

The Council's statement also makes clear that confirmation is not a single event but the beginning of a healing process that continues throughout our lives. It is important, for this reason, that every young person or adult who has been confirmed should be entrusted with duties that, to be carried out, really *need* the gifts that the Holy Spirit gives, so that they may experience the healing and strengthening effects of these gifts and be able to testify this to others. For example, it could prove very fruitful to place Bible groups and prayer circles under the leadership of newly confirmed teenagers and young adults, just *because* they are not given this duty simply on account of their intellectual abilities, but more especially to test the gifts of the Spirit that they have received.[4]

Practical works of charity also, such as visiting the old and the sick or contact with troubled young people, drug addicts, or alcoholics, for example, could be a blessing for the whole community if they are done in the first place as a witness to the power of the gifts received through the Spirit.[5] The healing effects of confirmation for the whole community will be difficult to see—and this is one reason why this sacrament is increasingly downplayed—as long as we hesitate to let those newly confirmed exercise the gifts they have received, under appropriate supervision. The Church as body of Christ can expect no healing of its members as long as it does not create a space for *spontaneous* works of charity also, which will complement the work of professionals. A fountain from which no one draws water any longer will get stopped up. If charity is usurped by social services, we kill any expectant faith in the healing power of the Spirit of God and, therefore, of those who have received the gifts of grace of the divine Spirit in the sacrament of confirmation—and not only for themselves and their own healing but precisely for service and witness to others as well.

Notes on Some Practices of the Renewal Movements

In those renewal movements without which we could no longer imagine the Church's life (Focolare, Cursillo, the charismatic movement, the neocatechumenate, the Schönstatt movement, and others), we find the same practices almost everywhere, bearing different names but serving one and the same function, namely, a step-by-step initiation and integration of believers into the movement, even in those groups which say they have no particular spirituality of their own. First we must be clear about the fact that, where these practices are known under such names as "baptism in the Spirit" or "renewal of confirmation," there is no question of new sacramental forms aimed at replacing and abolishing the existing ones. Their purpose is rather the actualization of those gifts of grace that the believers have already received when the sacraments (baptism and confirmation) were administered, but which, because of their youth in most cases, they were not able either to accept consciously or to apply in a meaningful way. Practically, the members pray in small groups with the initiates that they be filled with the Holy Spirit, requiring of them at the same time that they no longer seek to control their own lives but surrender themselves to the will of God in all things.

These practices can be extraordinarily fruitful both in the life of the individual and in that of the society or community. Of course, there are some conditions for this that may not always be fulfilled, sometimes because they are not perceived. First of all, it ought to be evident to all those concerned—and it should be clearly stated as well—that what is at stake in these practices is not a one-time event with guaranteed, lasting results. Rather, it is a matter of stages in an ongoing process of healing and sanctification that will not be perfected until physical death, namely, in the face-to-face encounter with the Savior.

It follows that these practices require, first, a time of fundamental preparation and, second, an equally intensive follow-up; in other words, they call for ongoing, personal support by people who are experienced and tested in the spiritual life. The preparation should not be restricted to a communication of knowledge about the sacraments and their graces with all the practical consequences of a life in the Holy Spirit; they should also include an exercise of those gifts. An absolutely necessary aspect of this is the removal of obstacles that prevent the coming of the Lord; by this I mean conscious and unconscious psychic blocks.

If that does not occur, the curious result may well be that being filled with the Holy Spirit, instead of being experienced as liberation, relief, and arming with spiritual strength, will seem an additional burden, complication, and often even a crippling weight. A young woman said to me: "I have already surrendered my life six times—and it just keeps getting worse!" Certainly, this supposed worsening cannot be the work of the Holy Spirit, but it is often laid at the Spirit's door. In reality, the Spirit of God not only frees positive strengths in human nature but also brings to light those that are less attractive, our "shadow sides," that appear all the darker the more light is directed on them. That in itself is a gift of grace, even if we experience it as just the opposite. For when these shadow sides are once brought into the light of consciousness, it is much easier to deal with them. They can no longer carry on their hide-and-seek game with us; they have to reveal themselves. But looking them in the eye in the full light of day can be painful. We experience it as anything but a gracious gift, and certainly not as the beginning of healing. Therefore it is preferable to work out serious spiritual problems *beforehand*, even if it takes time, patience, and nerve and, of course, demands a certain competence on the part of the support person.

Recognizing Our Dual Image of God

Let me mention, for example, just *one* problem whose many-faceted effects are all too often overlooked, although none of us is completely free of it: our often double-faced image of God. What do I mean by that, and what are its effects in us? Each of us, as a child, heard something about the "loving God" and we were happy to relate to this image. But perhaps this loving God was not *only* loving and good, perhaps God could also punish as our mother told us—namely, when we did not do what our mother said. Then we absorbed the thought: *you never know* how God will react at a given moment, for who has such a one-hundred-percent clear conscience that the loving God can never be anything but loving?

Maybe our mother used to talk a lot about the loving, good God, and our father tended to have sudden "explosions": not only did he suddenly begin to shout at us but he hit us as well. Then we got the picture of a God who is good and at the same time hands out blows, and whose love one would just as well do without; after all, who likes to be hit? And this mixture of conscious image of God (love) and unconscious idea of God (beatings) has usually shaped the child in us so enduringly that it remains determinative even for adults: we may like to talk a lot about God's love, but somehow (that is, unconsciously) we prefer not to let God get too close to us. . . . Of course, it may be that our father was devout and our mother irritable: they went directly from praying to yelling at us. Unfortunately, that is all too common—and it always has terrible effects on the (largely unconscious) image of God in the child's mind and leaves its deep marks on the adult. Worst of all for the child and its image of God, of course, is disharmony between the parents. No matter what pious words they use to try to conceal it from the children, those children will always carry in their hearts an image of the loving God who has both a green and a blue face, or is striped violet and pink from top to bottom. A religion teacher once had the courage to ask children of different ages to draw "father," "mother," "our family," and "the good and loving God." I have seldom seen a more terrible picture of the fragmentation of our inner life.

The problem with our image of God, however, is only one of many that make it difficult for us to surrender *totally* to God's direction, without provisos or conditions. And that is evidently what is meant when we speak of baptism in the Spirit, renewal of confirmation, surrender of our lives: it is always a matter of what the New Testament calls *metanoia*, namely, the turning of the whole person from this world and all its temptations and turning to the reign of God and the arming with the spiritual gifts needed for this way, gifts that can only come from a wholly personal and loving relationship with God.

Therefore it is better if we wrestle with the duality of our image of God and all its conscious and unconscious consequences for our spiritual and intellectual life *before* we surrender our lives *wholly* into God's hands. No matter how splintered our lives and our image of God may be, God can always heal us if we take enough time and trouble to cooperate. For it is from God (and from God alone) that we can know in faith that God is thoroughly and entirely good, because God is goodness itself.

Notes

1. Decree on the Apostolate of the Laity, 3.

2. Constitution on the Liturgy *(Sacrosanctum Concilium,* hereafter abbreviated *SC)* 61.

3. Decree on the Apostolate of the Laity, 3.

4. "Through the Holy Spirit the weak become strong, the poor become rich, the dependent and uneducated wiser than the learned. Paul was weak, but because of the presence of the Spirit the hand-

kerchiefs that touched his body brought healing to those who took them. Peter also had a weak body, but thanks to the grace of the Spirit that dwelt in him, the shadow of his body drove out the illness of those who were suffering. Peter and John were poor, for they had neither silver nor gold; but they gave health, which is worth more than gold. That lame man received money from many persons, but still remained a beggar; yet when he received Peter's gift, he leapt up like a stag, praised God and ceased to beg. John knew nothing of the wisdom of this world, and yet he spoke in the power of the Spirit's word, to which no wisdom can attain.'' (Basil the Great, ''Sermon on Faith,'' 3).

5. See, on this point, the practical experiences with newly confirmed people related by Fr. Michael Scanlan in *Their Eyes were Opened*, 67–75.

FIVE

Healing Through the Eucharist

Well hidden in the new texts of the Mass, like an image in one of those "find it" pictures, is an old prayer that may provide the key to the Eucharistic celebration as sacrament of healing. After Communion in the Body and Blood of Christ, the priest is to pray: "Lord, may [these gifts] . . . bring me healing and strength, now and for ever." According to one of the many rubrics in the altar missal, the priest is supposed to pray this *inaudibly*, and in the newest missal for private use it is set in such small type, and surrounded by so much red, that one really has to wonder if any believer has ever heard or read it. That is very sad. For this prayer echoes the words of St. Ignatius of Antioch, whom I already mentioned in the chapter on baptism because of his intrepid faith. Thus it is one of the oldest and most precious of the Church's treasures of faith. Ignatius calls the Eucharist "medicine for immortality," and also "a medicine against death."

A formulation very similar in meaning, as regards the healing power of the Eucharist, is also to be found in the documents of Vatican Council II, where we read that the Eucharist is "a pledge of future glory."[1] It is thus something that lifts a human person out of the limitations of earthly life into the realm of eternity. This should be regarded as an ongoing process in the life of a Christian and of the Church, something that is continually needed because individuals repeatedly cut themselves off from the gifts of salvation that were received in the sacrament of baptism, that is, from their initial liberation from the powers of darkness and the realm of evil. The celebration of the Eucharist continues this process of our liberation, begun in baptism and strengthened in confirmation, because it is not merely the remembering of a single historical event, but, as the Council says, it "perpetuate[s] the sacrifice of the Cross throughout the centuries"[2]—it constitutes in itself a process of salvation history through the working of the Holy Spirit. Of course, it not only involves liberation from the *temporal* limitations of our earthly life but also and at the same time promotes growth into a new dimension of human relationships.

"We become what we receive: the Body of Christ," said St. Augustine. In other words: we encounter one another in a different way, on a different level; we are no longer simply dependent on criteria such as "likable" or "unappealing"; we no longer judge others according to their appearance, wealth, and achievements—by what they have and what they can do—but first of all according to what they are. They can be poorly dressed, not good-looking, perhaps physically or mentally handicapped—they may even be repulsive—and suddenly or gradually, through the celebration of the Eucharist, I will discover that this or that person is beautiful: I begin to catch glimpses of their inner beauty to which I was blind before. The eyes of my heart will be opened, because sin has lost its power over me. "Sin clouds the spirit; it closes the eyes of the heart," as the Curé of Ars said.

How can this happen in practice? What can believers contribute to their own healing through the celebration of the Eucharist? Vatican Council II says that the Eucharistic sacrifice is offered by the participation of *all* believers, not just by the priest. *Each* one should offer his or her *whole* life. The presence of Christ through the Holy Spirit, and not only in his Body and Blood but also in the community of the faithful, brings about the community of human beings with God, their Father, and with one another. So they "should be drawn day by day into ever closer union with God and with each other, so that finally God may be all in all."[3]

But Christ the mediator, as head of the body, brings about a union not only of the assembled community as members of one body with one another but also of the *whole* Church of all times and nations, the Church in heaven and the Church on earth. For *all* belong to the *one* body, whose head is Christ and whose members we are. He offered his life ''for you and for all.''

What We May and Should Expect

This unity of the body through the unique sacrifice of Christ is important for the attitude we bring to the celebration of the Eucharist. What do we expect when we ''go to church''? What do we bring with us besides our expectations? Don't we too often regard the Church as a kind of service facility, which we support at a rather high price and from which we are entitled to expect a correspondingly high quality of work in return? Are we not in a sense *obligated* to be sure that the Church uses our money responsibly and to criticize what seems to us to be deficient? Can we let the pastors say and do whatever is currently in fashion?

But we could put a different set of questions: why is there so little wholeness, so little health in our churches? Or still more pointedly: why are so few people healed in our church services? Why aren't the *others* being healed—and why am *I* not being healed? Why isn't there even reconciliation and forgiveness among us? Do I realize that the Church not only prays for ''salvation'' (some salvation or other for someone or other, one is tempted to say), but that in *every* Eucharistic celebration we really, *expressly* pray for the salvation and healing of *every* person—therefore for *my* salvation and *my* healing? And do I realize that I may and should expect to receive this salvation and healing?—not, of course, as a magical event that functions by the touch of some invisible button and to which I am entitled because I come regularly and punctually.

God can and will heal through the sacrament of the Eucharist to the extent that I bring my whole life into the celebration in *expectant faith* within the community of the Church, that is, together with *all* people from every time and nation—and to the extent that I leave it to God how God will heal me and what consequences that healing will have for my life. If we expect anything at all, our expectations are all too often connected with some very fixed ideas about what ought to change in our lives and what consequences the change ought to have—and we are disappointed if just this change, improvement, or healing does not come about. In fact, in our bitter disappointment we may even overlook a healing that has really happened because it was much more urgent than the one we hoped for. I actually experienced, at a Eucharistic celebration, the healing of someone who suffered from chronic depression, but the person in question did not want to acknowledge this healing, which changed her life from the ground up, because some minor headaches, which she had "counted on" getting rid of, remained for the moment unchanged.

What kind of healing can we expect, then, from the celebration of the Eucharist? First let us speak about the attitude of the priest and that of the believers toward the priest. The priest stands at the altar *in persona Christi*, in the place of Christ. For that reason alone he needs the continuing prayers of the faithful. But by the same token, the function of the believers is not restricted to that of more or less critical observers, since, according to the Council, "Christ's faithful, when present at this mystery of faith, should not be there as strangers or silent spectators. On the contrary, through a proper appreciation of the rites and prayers they should participate knowingly, devoutly and actively . . . [and thus] they should learn to offer themselves too."[4] *All*, together with the priest, are therefore to offer the Eucharistic sacrifice in order to experience salvation and healing together. This means for the priest that the more faithfully he adheres to the obligatory liturgical texts, which are identical throughout the world, in loving obedience to Jesus and the Church, the greater will be the healing and sanctifying power that will pour into the body of Christ as the fruit of its oneness and harmonic unanimity.[5]

The healing effect of the Eucharist certainly does *not* result, then, from the personal charisma of this or that priest, nor from the pedagogical ambitions of the local liturgical commission. It does not even flow from the special gifts of grace bestowed on a particular priest and the resulting expectations of the faithful. The healing effect of the Eucharist results solely from the consciousness on the part of both priest and people of their own poverty and lowliness, from their willingness to be nothing more than instruments and recipients; to put it more plainly, from their knowledge of their total unworthiness and dependence with which, together, they await the coming of their Lord and Savior when they pray: "Lord, I am not worthy to receive you, but only say the word, and I shall be healed." Because this Word is the Word that became *flesh*, it is not so remarkable that, in the Eucharist celebrated in a spirit of expectant faith, we may experience not only spiritual but physical healing. The greatest gift, of course, remains that of everlasting life—abolition of the limitedness and vulnerability of our earthly life as a result of original sin.

Dangers of Consumerist Attitude

For that reason there are a number of dangers in the attitudes of believers at the Eucharistic celebration that ought to be mentioned. Just as extreme as the attitude of expecting nothing at all from the Eucharist is the opposite one of trying to fixate God and the priest on the relief of a particular symptom (or, more precisely, to tie oneself down to this *single* expectation)—and accordingly, to be disappointed when what we are praying for does not happen. Behind both attitudes is a secular consumerist attitude that we unwittingly carry over into the liturgy. On the one hand, I tell myself that I have nothing to give—so what could I expect to receive? On the other hand, I think that the simple fact that I am present ("fulfilling my Sunday obligation") entitles me to choose whatever I please: *I* decide how well the choir sang, whether the pastor gave a good homily, what was not "done" properly in the course of the liturgy—and of course, whether the healing I expected has been granted in exactly the way I imagined. Everything is supposed to be "right"—it doesn't occur to me at all that I might contribute something without immediately expecting something in return. Even less do I imagine that *every* gift of God, no matter how grand or how modest it may be, is always an *undeserved* gift—and that I can do absolutely *nothing* except to receive it in humility and joy. Whether I have come expecting nothing, my heart and mind full of criticism toward everything that goes on, or whether I make an honest effort to open myself in expectant faith to the event and thus to contribute my part to the "success" of the liturgy—in either case I must always be aware that I am and always will be a "worthless servant." But recognizing that and accepting it with a spark of humor is precisely what is often so hard for us. Nevertheless, it is the first and most essential precondition for healing to happen at all: that I can accept a gift of God *for its own sake*, and not because of some kind of return favor on my part.

Surrender of One's Self-Images

A further decisive precondition that is almost as difficult for me to accept is "to surrender my life," or as the Council says, "to offer the Eucharist together with the priest." What does that mean? How is it supposed to happen in practice? Surrendering one's life certainly does not mean becoming replaceable, as many of us fear. What we think is our personality is often precisely *not* that unique and irreplaceable thing for which God made us, but the replaceable, that in us which is subject to all the trends, something we have "acquired" for ourselves; not just our clothes and cars but also certain personal images that each of us depends upon to a greater or lesser extent. Anyone who wants to be a politician has to wear a certain kind of glasses or not be elected. If someone wants to be president or CEO of a company, she or he had better not go to church on Sundays; that doesn't fit the image. There are statistical studies of these things which in turn create their own trends.

But God does not create trends: God creates people. And God does not desire that these people sink in the flood of their guilt feelings, whether these feelings are appropriate or are for those things of which they only think they are guilty. God wants the drowning person to surface and *live*. That is why God became human, in order to free us from everything that we are *not:* what people tell us we ought to be in order to be more manipulable and to spend more money on things that we neither need nor want, to seem more and be less, to estrange ourselves more and more from what we really are, what we were made to be—not to run around like confused sheep in wolf's clothing, homeless, without belonging anywhere and with no ground beneath our feet but instead to be children of God who live in the freedom of God's children.

To surrender our life thus does not mean to throw it away, to dispossess ourselves or become expendable, but on the contrary, to accept the gift of that life for which the Father made us and the Son redeemed us—and that makes superfluous every other life I have been persuaded to try. To surrender one's life is not some lovely theory, but a very practical problem: I cannot accept the gift of a new heart of flesh and blood as long as I am not prepared to give up my heart of stone: what I thought my life was, up until now.

Healing: A Conscious Process

This process of change and healing in me is, of course, not restricted to a few moments or high points in the liturgy; it goes on during the *entire* celebration of the Eucharist, from the opening words to the closing blessing. In a sense it begins when I take holy water and cross myself as a recollection of my baptism, and when I again make the Sign of the Cross together with the priest and all the faithful, saying: "In the name of the Father and of the Son and of the Holy Spirit." For even at that moment I am delivered from the realm of the power of evil and may consciously allow myself to be incorporated in the reign of God. This process of healing which is already beginning is given expression when the priest prays: "Lord Jesus, you were sent by the Father to heal what is wounded," and all answer: "Lord, have mercy." Our healing thus begins with the first words and signs of the Eucharistic liturgy. It is certainly not unimportant that, with a gesture—the Sign of the Cross—we include our bodies and senses in the holy actions: the *whole* human person with *all* its aspects should be subject to healing and salvation through Jesus, the Savior and Redeemer. But we need to make our contribution to these actions through our active and conscious participation. That is the dignity and coresponsibility of the human being as a creature, made in the image of the Creator. It also belongs to this dignity and coresponsibility of the human being as creature to acknowledge freely his or her dependence on the Creator and on the Creator's mercy that has become human in Jesus. Therefore it is no slavish attitude, but the expression of our trust when we confess in words and signs that we *need* Jesus as our Savior to deliver us from sin: "You were sent by the Father to heal what is wounded," and when we also clearly acknowledge our dependence on this divine mercy: "Lord, have mercy."

Thus the Church does not intend to "put us down," humiliate us, or berate our consciences; instead, it simply wants to give us a chance at healing through a sober demonstration of facts, when in the whole course of the Eucharistic liturgy it confronts us with our sinfulness in an increasing crescendo— but at the same time shows us the constantly multiplying offer of salvation. The intensity with which we really profit by the offer of healing and salvation that is made to us will depend on our insight into our need for that wholeness.

Necessity of Worthy Proclamation

The proclamation of the Word of God that follows the initial rite of penitence is a continuation of the healing process.

It is the Word that became flesh, God's salvation that took on a human form and desires to reveal itself to us in all imaginable dimensions, variations, and nuances that in any way belong to humanity. Always and everywhere, the Word of God is about our salvation—even and especially where it is most drastically clear where our weakness lies and what is necessary for our conversion. The way in which the Word of God is proclaimed is largely contributory to its *healing* effect. A message that is droned out like a weather report, perhaps with mistakes or emphases that distort the sense but in any case without the lector's having any relationship to the inner meaning of the Word being proclaimed, cannot have any healing effect. At the most, its effect is embarrassing and serves only to increase the pain of the congregation instead of easing it.[6] If the lectors do not first let themselves be touched, penetrated, and grasped by the healing and saving effect of the Word, they cannot expect that their proclamation of the Word will have any healing or saving effect on the faithful. Lectors need to take time for preparation, for inner dialogue with the text and for becoming well acquainted with it, and finally, time for its proclamation. That is true both for the first reading or readings and for the gospel—and all the more, of course, for their unfolding in the homily.[7]

The new missal expressly provides that the deacon should ask the priest for the following blessing, so that he may appropriately proclaim the gospel: "The Lord be in your heart and on your lips that you may worthily proclaim his gospel. In the name of the Father, and of the Son, and of the Holy Spirit."

After the proclamation of the gospel, the deacon or priest should pray: "May the words of the gospel wipe away our sins." Both the important and profound blessing *before* and the prayer *after* the gospel, which is so decisive for the healing effect of the Word of God, should, according to the directions in the missal, be spoken *in a low voice*. That is regrettable. In this way we conceal from the faithful that the Church really places great value on a worthy proclamation, because this

Word in itself, namely, as the revelation of God's love, has in an especially intense degree the power to deliver from sin and thus to heal. The Latin prayer after the reading expresses this trust of the Church in the healing Word of God even more succinctly: "Per evangelia dicta, deleantur nostra delicta."

Necessity of Trust

If the Word is read and received with that kind of trust, it can effect not only spiritual but also physical cures. I have seen how an unusually persistent skin rash began to improve, not at the prayer for healing at the end of the Mass but during the Liturgy of the Word—and by the end of the celebration was almost completely cured. Here the Word become flesh had literally touched a human being and changed that person's life. For in this case the physical healing brought with it a spiritual change as well.

After the proclamation of the Word of God, the gifts are prepared. The priest prays over the bread and wine a prayer that Jesus might have spoken at the Last Supper. It is part of the oldest tradition of the Jewish liturgy and is prayed even today in every Jewish home as a table blessing. Literally translated, it says: "Blessed art thou, Eternal One, Ruler of the World, who causes bread to grow from the earth/who causes the vine to spring forth."[8]

When Jesus later says of this bread: "This is my body. Take, all of you, and eat of it," he returns the Father's gift of life. He knows that, like all creation, his life is nothing but a gift of the Father to the Son—and thus to all humanity. As the Son of Humanity, Jesus offers this gift to his divine Father. He gives it back, consciously and freely, into the hands of the Father. It is through his loving obedience as a human being that he saves human persons and frees them from sin, from their separation from God resulting from lack of obedience—more precisely, from an original human mistrust of God's love. Jesus heals human beings from this original mistrust by the confident surrender of his being into the Father's protection. That means concretely that he heals *every* human being at *every* celebration of the Eucharist from this original, native lack of trust—insofar as that person is prepared to open him- or herself to God in expectant faith. Not only are the gifts of bread and wine prepared and transformed into the Body and Blood of Christ, but with them also the gift of the life of each person is transformed into a God-like life in purity and freedom. The human being is freed and healed from sin and its manifold wounds and stains.

So far as appearances are concerned, life remains as it was. Only rarely does a visible and perceptible change occur during the Mass. Reports of exceptional "spiritual experiences" at the Eucharist ought to be treated with caution. And yet, at *every* celebration of the Eucharist, for *every* person, there occurs a quite decisive change of his or her whole being (however little it may be subjectively perceived): the individual and the community of the body of Christ are really lifted out of the realm of the power of evil and brought within the reign of God. All those walls of pride, hate, envy, rivalry, and every kind of mistrust that have been built by the arrogance of human beings can fall. We may see ourselves and others with the eyes of the heart: created by the Father, redeemed by the Son, and temples of the Holy Spirit. "You were bought at a great price," says the apostle Paul, namely the price of the precious blood of Christ. This redemption makes up the greatness and worth of *each* individual human being—this, and not his or her achievements or wealth. All our blinders made up of pride or feelings of inferiority become superfluous. Our view expands beyond all limits. The presence of God is visible in every human person.

That certainly does not mean that everyone will be perfected simply by taking part in the Eucharist. But our imperfection is relativized in view of the absolute. God is the absolute Good and Perfect One. Whatever divides us, limits us, and separates us from one another has no power, or only very limited power, in face of God's absolute goodness.

For this divine goodness is precisely *not* a demonstration

of power: in the surrender of his flesh and blood "for love of his friends," he stands before us in all his pitifulness, abandonment, degradation, and dependence on our kindness. What God will be in this world depends on us; whether the reality of God's presence is still persuasive, whether it is still effective, whether it can still change something in human life, really depends on us, on the witness of *our* lives, the testimony of *our* transformation through the celebration of the Eucharist.

The various Eucharistic prayers unfold the many dimensions of what has happened in the consecration. They meditate both on the meaning of Christ's sacrifice for all humanity in salvation history and on its meaning for the present.

The Universal Dimension of Healing

Since their content is God's saving action for Christ's mystical body, the Church, these central prayers of Christian faith are also healing prayers in the most comprehensive sense of the word. It is always a matter of God's love and deepest desire for reconciliation of human persons with God and one another. We may take as just one example among many a single phrase from the Third Eucharistic Prayer: ". . . in mercy and love unite all your children wherever they may be." This prayer contains not only a missionary idea, that through the mercy of God those, too, should be brought together who do not know God or have distanced themselves from God, but especially the petition that God, in the Son, would reconcile those who, in spite of all human effort, could not be moved to reconciliation. Of course, that cannot happen unless we are willing also to forgive those who have hurt us or who are still persecuting us. And it cannot happen without our readiness to be reconciled with those who have excluded themselves by their own fault. As long as I am not prepared to approach my "enemy," the whole body of Christ will suffer from it. It will not be able either to heal or to be salvation for others. "So if you are offering your gift at the altar, and there remember that your brother has something against you, leave your gift there before the altar and go; first be reconciled to your brother, and then come and offer your gift" (Matt 5:23-24). As long as I exclude *one* person from my prayers, the Eucharistic celebration will not really be "catholic," that is, universal: encompassing the whole world and including the whole body of Christ. On the other hand, however, reconciliation and, therefore, healing too can occur just there where I am prepared in principle to take the first step but do not consider it possible that the other is equally ready to do so. That is by no means a reason to hesitate or despair: what I think is impossible because I cannot imagine it is far from being impossible for God.[9]

After the Eucharistic prayer comes the Communion rite, beginning with the Our Father. The only condition attached to the fulfillment of *all* the petitions in the Lord's Prayer is again *our* forgiveness of sins: "And forgive us our trespasses, as we forgive those who trespass against us." A number of early manuscripts have: ". . . as we *have forgiven* those who trespass against us." That is, we cannot let it rest with the pious petition; God can only forgive us after we have forgiven one another. This corresponds to the oldest Jewish tradition: on the Day of Atonement even Almighty God can only forgive as much guilt as I have already forgiven my neighbor. But there is the fulfillment of the other petitions in the Our Father as well: the hallowing of God's name, the coming of the reign of God and the carrying out of God's will, and even our having enough to eat each day are all made dependent on our willingness to forgive each other's sins. Without our own personal readiness for peace and reconciliation there will be no peace and no reconciliation in the world. Neither in heaven nor on earth can God do anything unless we do our part.

Of course, God has to deliver us from the evil in us and outside us—and this petition is then taken up, repeated, and intensified: "Deliver us, Lord, from every evil and give peace in our day. In your mercy keep us free from sin and protect us from all anxiety as we wait in joyful hope for the coming of our Savior, Jesus Christ." Here we can see the urgency with which the Church implores the salvation of its faithful. Confusion is one of evil's most powerful weapons. We avoid clarity and light, especially at the point where our bad conscience presses upon us and wants to hold us captive. We prefer complicated detours—often cloaked in the most devout practices—just to avoid recognizing and acknowledging our sins. But in that way we often detour around Christ's saving and healing power. A peaceful simplicity and permanency—which is something quite different from peace at any price—are among the most effective means for combating evil's confusing games with their high-flying, more-or-less spiritual abstractions.

The Church wants to lead us again and again to this decisive and conscious simplicity and clarity by having us confess and proclaim the reign and the power and the glory of *God*, and thus to prepare us for the confession of God's peace.

The sign of peace can be one of the central gestures within the Eucharistic celebration as a whole, if it is exchanged consciously and seriously. The priest invites us with the words: "Give *one another* a sign of peace and reconciliation." Thus, peace and reconciliation do not remain simply pious wishes on the part of the priest; the dignity and responsibility of transmitting to one another that peace and forgiveness that come from the Lord's cross and from his precious blood are conferred upon *everyone* present.[10]

This can be done in a simple and yet impressive manner by extending both hands to one's neighbor on the right and on the left. We are so familiar with this gesture of handshaking that we seldom reflect consciously on its meaning, which goes back to the Middle Ages: when a conflict between two knights and their followers had been settled, they first put up their visors in order to look one another in the eye again, and then threw away their iron gloves, showing and extending both hands to one another as a sign that neither bore a weapon or a grudge against the other any longer. This was intended primarily to express the peace in their hearts. We find quite often that, through this simple gesture during the celebration of the Eucharist, people who beforehand were not at all ready to surrender their prejudices against one another are now able to do so. This willingness for reconciliation can then lead, among other things, to healing of physical ailments which had baffled medical treatment. A religious who had had a knee stiffened for years by arthritis was astonished to discover, in being reconciled with another member of her community, that she had been so spontaneously healed that she could kneel again without any pain.

"My servant will be healed"

The Eucharist reaches its high point of healing power with the Communion and the prayers that accompany it before and afterward. Some of these are specific requests for healing. It is unfortunate that the priest is supposed to speak the prayer of preparation for Communion *inaudibly*, because in that way it remains concealed from the people. "Lord Jesus Christ, with faith in your love and mercy I eat your body and drink your blood. Let it not bring me condemnation, but health in mind and body."[11]

In addition, the somewhat longer prayer of preparation which the priest can choose in place of the prayer just quoted is basically a prayer for healing, although somewhat less expressly so: "Lord Jesus Christ, Son of the living God, by the will of the Father and the work of the Holy Spirit your death brought life to the world. By your holy body and blood free me from all my sins and from every evil. Keep me faithful to your teaching and never let me be parted from you." Here it is a matter, first of all, of salvation to everlasting life and deliverance from sin and evil, as well as the preservation of this present life through continuance in the presence of God, the source of all life; but at the same time it is a question of the healing of the whole person, including the body.

After this the priest shows the Body of Christ to the people and says: "This is the Lamb of God who takes away the sin of the world." It is not by divine strength that God heals and transforms the world, but precisely through divine weakness. Perhaps we are so habituated to hearing these words that we are no longer shocked by the difficulty of such a statement for our minds, which are so molded by the spirit of this world: what an absurd idea, that a lamb should prove stronger than all the horrors of this world, including Auschwitz and "Star Wars." Only after our understanding has, so to speak, blood-ied itself on this thorn can we perhaps begin to glimpse how much healing power for all humanity is concealed in this *mystery of faith*. What will always remain inaccessible to our senses and understanding need not therefore be less real and less effective. It is the most inward reality that can be. We have the opportunity every day to smirk at this mystery or to reject it as a massive affront to our reason—or to open ourselves to the reality with the speechless astonishment of the child, who knows better what is happening here than does the adult in us. We should always be aware at the same time that this opening of oneself to the mystery can only happen slowly, that it involves a lifelong process, until one day our reason is prepared to "knuckle under." Only then can our healing be perfected—when we can view the Savior face to face—at the moment of our physical death.

Immediately before Communion we pray: "Lord, I am not worthy to receive you; only say the word and I shall be healed." That is certainly the expression of the utmost trust in the reality of the divine mystery—and thus also in the effectiveness of its healing power.

Of course, it is the healing of the *whole* person that is meant here as well. In the gospel the phrase is: "my *servant* will be healed"—that is, the human person—body, psyche, and spirit. For the *one* word is nothing other than the Word that has become flesh—flesh of our flesh—and thereby it has already saved everything earthly and mortal in us, redeemed and healed it for eternal life.

Finally, in Communion this one Word that became flesh enters totally, with his own body, into our bodies. Irenaeus of Lyons, a second-century Church Father, was convinced that in this way our bodies are changed into his. Let us not be too quick to smile at that kind of "prescientific thinking"! Irenaeus was writing against those heretics who did not want to accept the incarnation and its consequences for the redemption of our bodies and who did not believe that we are called to eternal life and to bodily resurrection with Jesus, the head of that mystical body whose members we are. Irenaeus wrote:

> And vain altogether are they, who despise God's entire plan, and deny the salvation of the flesh and scorn its new birth, saying that it cannot receive incorruption. . . . Since therefore both the cup which is mingled and the bread which is made receive the Word of God, and the Eucharist becomes the body of Christ, from which the substance of our flesh grows and subsists, how can they [the heretics] say that flesh is not capable of the gift of God, which is eternal life—that flesh which is nourished by the body and blood of the Lord, and is a member of him? . . . So are our bodies also nourished from it [the Eucharist] and when they are put into the ground, and dissolved in it, they shall rise again in their own time, when the Word of God gives them resurrection to the glory of God the Father. He wins immortality for that which is mortal, and on that which is corruptible freely bestows incorruption, because the power of God is made perfect in weakness. . . . So experience should teach us that we endure forever because of his greatness, and not by the strength of our own nature.[12]

"What God Has Promised"

If our bodies are so penetrated by the Body of Christ, it is not really very remarkable but simply a proof of the love of God that we may expect and experience even physical healing at Communion. The Church expresses this expectation in a number of concluding prayers to be said after Communion. In this way it shows its confidence that God "is able to do what God has promised" (Rom 4:21). It is certainly no accident that it is especially in the liturgy before and after Easter, at the time when the Church celebrates most intensively the suffering and resurrection of its Lord, that the concluding prayers very often expressly ask for physical healing. For example, on the first Thursday in Lent we pray: "Lord our God, renew us by these

mysteries. May they heal us now and bring us eternal salvation," and on Thursday of the second week of Easter:
"Strengthen us by this Easter sacrament, may we feel its saving power in our daily life."

If the Church prays so naturally and expressly for the healing of the *whole* person, then as I have said, we need not think
it so remarkable but only a sign of the mercy and love of our
God when we have experiences like this one—I offer it as just
one example among many—which took place after Communion at a Eucharistic celebration in a small group: a religious
who was preparing to take thirty schoolchildren to camp the
next day had had such a bad fall on the staircase that the doctor found a severe hemorrhage in her knee and ordered her
to rest the leg completely for the next two weeks. But that
would have meant no camp for the thirty children! So we
simply thanked the Lord for having healed us in body and
spirit through the sacrament of the Eucharist—and the next day
the sister set off for camp with her thirty children, free of pain
and in good spirits. Two weeks later she wrote: "I thank the
Lord not only for physical healing, but even more that he has
healed me from my ties to a person from whom I had no longer
hoped to free myself." It was a revelation of God's power to
do what God had promised. We should expect nothing less
at *every* Eucharistic celebration. Therefore it is important that
the priest, either in the homily or at some other point, should
always point out the healing dimension of the Mass. It is just
as important that after the Communion he should permit a long
period of silence in which each individual and all together may
give thanks for healing. If Communion in the body and blood
of Christ means more to us than an oral vaccination, and if
we can expect more from it than magical effects, we need this
silence in which to receive the Lord into our lives like a familiar guest—and to thank him for being with us and healing us
through nothing but his presence. This moment after Communion is a time of tenderness that we should not surrender
(and that should not be disturbed by the priest's activities at
the altar or by the organist or choir). In this silence, again and

again, just those healings and conversions that no one had consciously expected may be given. Without knowing it, *everyone* comes to *every* liturgy filled with hope—otherwise they would not come at all. But such indications of God's grace are often nipped in the bud if there is *no* silence at all after Communion or if it is much too short; if the service moves too quickly and loudly toward its conclusion.

The concluding prayer can only give grateful emphasis to the healing that has already happened in Communion. But for just that reason—namely, because it is a thanksgiving and confirmation—it is by no means unimportant or superfluous. Here the priest should also have the freedom to elaborate on the confidence in healing that has happened in prayer, a confidence that the Church expresses in any case. He should not try to introduce anything at all new but simply acknowledge, in astonishment and gratitude, all that may have happened and really has happened in the way of visible and invisible healings in the body, psyche, and spirit of each individual.

The final blessing then acts as a summation of all the gifts received during the whole Eucharistic celebration. At the same time it means that those who are blessed should become a blessing. Thus the priest's "Go in peace," is not just a friendly dismissal. It was from this phrase ("Ite, missa est") that the Mass took its name: the *whole* Eucharist should be a celebration of sending forth. The peace we have received from the Lord—purchased by his precious blood—is for us to hand on so that others may share in the salvation that has thus become ours. Vatican Council II says that the Eucharist is the source and summit of all *evangelization*.[13] The message of his death and resurrection, which we have not only heard but absorbed into our lives, is to be communicated to others as *the* message of his and our peace, of his and our love.

Notes

1. SC 47.
2. *Ibid.*

3. *Ibid.*, 48.

4. *Ibid.*

5. I was ordained a priest in 1968, and experimentation with the new liturgy was thus commonplace for me from the beginning. It was only my constant contact with sick people that convinced me, by experience, that the more sober and true to the text the Eucharistic celebration is, the more intensive will be its healing effect. I do not mean to say anything against efforts at inculturation, i.e., the adaptation of the Roman rite to the cultures of other continents. In the course of many visits abroad I have learned to value these efforts greatly.

6. I really hardly know whether to laugh or cry when I hear proclaimed, during Holy Week, with great ceremony, that Jesus' feet were anointed with genuine "lard."

7. I am often asked how the faithful are supposed to know what healing power is hidden in the celebration of the sacraments, especially in *every* Eucharistic celebration. The answer is simple: someone should tell them. Concretely, the homily in particular should be used to point toward the hidden treasures of the Eucharist, as well as the other sacraments.

8. The added phrase, "through the work of human hands" is not in the original.

9. The brothers Dennis and Matthew Linn, S.J., write in their book, *Healing Life's Hurts: Healing Memories Through Five Stages of Forgiveness* (New York: Paulist Press, 1978) about a seminar for divorced people who were brought to the point of being able to forgive their former partners. Within eight days, eighty percent of those partners, who knew nothing about this seminar, and many of whom had not been heard from for a long time, reopened contact with their former spouses.

10. In the Dominican liturgy the priest, before giving the sign of peace, kisses the edge of the chalice containing the precious blood, in order to make clear that it is the *Lord's* peace that the priest gives to the faithful.

11. It is perplexing to note that the words "mind and body," which are so important for the healing of the *whole* person, are retained in the Latin original but are missing from the official German translation.

12. Irenaeus of Lyons, *Against Heresies* 5, 2, 2-3.

13. *SC* 15.

SIX

Healing Through the Sacrament of Reconciliation

Nothing is so painful as hurting someone when I know that person loves me. Such a one is completely vulnerable, and I strike him or her in the heart. "Why do you give me such pain when I love you so much," the Curé of Ars heard God saying. And in his distress he cried to his parishioners: "We are fleeing from our beloved and throwing ourselves into the arms of the executioner!"

Sin is murder, then! More exactly, it is suicide. For the murderer is no one but oneself. "You need a miracle to save a soul like that," the Curé of Ars said of a person who had committed a grave sin, "and a greater miracle than the raising of Lazarus." Here again, sin is equated with death, and deliverance from sin with being raised to new life. Jesus does the same in the parable of the prodigal son. "My son was dead and is alive again," Jesus has the father cry; "he was lost, and is found!" (cf. Luke 15:32).

"I would be glad to go to confession, but I haven't committed any sins." Priests often hear this statement nowadays. Apparently there are many people today who no longer have any consciousness of what sin really means, or of what importance sin ought to have in their lives—what they have to do with it at all. "Something is wrong with me," they say, and many are filled with guilt feelings that poison and burden their lives. In the opinion of more than a few people, they need a good, capable psychologist.

How could the Curé of Ars, one of the greatest confessors in all Europe—how, in fact, could Jesus—say that sin had something to do with death, that it is murder, even suicide? The English word "sin" is supposed to come from a root meaning to cut (oneself) off. Adam and Eve cut themselves off from God as the source of their life when the snake whispered to them: "You will be like God." In other words, you don't need anyone else, you can live by and for yourselves, in fact it is better that way than with someone on whom you will always be dependent. This temptation to independence conveys something very important: sin presupposes a relationship, a very lively one—the relationship to life itself—that has to be broken so that death may enter. Without a loving relationship with God there can be no consciousness of sin. Without being aware of this loving relationship with God as the Creator of my life, I cannot recognize sin, the divorce from this Creator of life, as death. That is why so many say that they have not committed sin or are not aware of any sins: because they have no loving relationship with God. They are not aware how they might have given God pain. How should I give injury to someone to whom I am in no way connected? Sin is the deadly wound given to a loving relationship. Nothing hurts more than wounding the beloved. It has to seem like my own death to me; it kills the love that keeps me alive.

So the question arises: how can this deadly wound be healed, or can it be healed at all? What are the means—unless a miracle should happen, as the saintly Curé of Ars said? The answer is simple: there are no means; a miracle *does* have to happen: the miracle of our healing, in fact, of our resurrection. This "miracle" happens in confession, or as the Church now calls it, the sacrament of reconciliation.

But *how* does it happen? To begin with, the Latin word *confessio* (literally: confession, acknowledgment) does not mean first of all the confession of my sins, but first and primarily the acknowledgment of the perfection and greatness of God—

and because of that the confession of my own imperfection, especially of my lack of love for God.

This imperfection of mine is certainly an offense and insult to God who made me in the divine image and wants me to be perfect as God is. But how in particular do I give pain to God? By injuring myself, God's creation! "God desires the good of human persons," said St. Thomas Aquinas. It is just because human beings hurt themselves, even kill themselves by cutting themselves off from the Creator of life, that they drag their God into suffering (com-passion) with them; and the two need reconciliation through Jesus, the Son who is fully God and fully human. He came in order to eradicate Adam's disobedience and separation through his own loving obedience.

"The Wound of Sin"

The sacrament of our reconciliation with the Father was instituted by Jesus when he, as the Son, took our sins on himself. "For our sake [the Father] made him to be sin who knew no sin, so that in him we might become the righteousness of God," says Paul (2 Cor 5:21). In this way, by our entry into the righteousness of God, the sacrament of reconciliation has become in a special way a sacrament of healing, for the "righteousness of God" is, for Paul, practically the same thing as the "glory of God." We are liberated and healed from everything that separates us from God.

Vatican Council II gives special emphasis to this healing aspect of the sacrament of reconciliation. In the introduction to the new rite of reconciliation we read that the person being reconciled "through the corresponding remedy [is] cured of the sickness from which he [she] suffered" (no. 6). And in another place: "Just as the wound of sin is varied and multiple in the life of individuals and of the community, so too the healing which penance provides is varied" (no. 7).

The same introduction also presents a new term for a reality which in itself is nothing new in the Church's consciousness, but which had in large measure been lost in our practice of confession and needed to be brought back to our awareness. It is the reality which the Church today summarizes in the concept of "the wound of sin." What does that mean? By the damage done to their loving relationship with God, sinners not only give pain to God but also to themselves. In most cases they incur not only spiritual wounds but also psychic and sometimes even physical distress. And these in turn affect not only the life of each individual but also those of his or her family, parish, or religious community. It is precisely these effects that the Church refers to as "the wound of sin."

For example: someone suffers from feelings of inferiority. That is a sin, because such a person does not have enough confidence in her or his beauty and dignity, as one created in the image of God, redeemed by the Son, and temple of the Holy Spirit. This sin, namely, the inferiority complex, will cause a wound that reveals itself in the person's constantly having to do and say things that make him or her appear better than she or he really thinks is right. Such a person gives the impression of being arrogant or deceitful, and is certainly irritating. She or he will always be trying to attract attention: "People show off because they need to," as the Berliners say. But it gets on the nerves of one's spouse, parish council, prayer group, religious superior. The dissatisfaction will spread, the wounds will expand, the sickness will become infectious. How can blood poisoning, or even an epidemic be prevented? Through confession, in which the confessor and the penitent are both aware not only of the sin but of the wounds of sin. The Church itself expresses its awareness of the necessity of healing both aspects—sin and the wounds of sin—in the new formula of absolution: "Through the ministry of the church may God give you pardon and peace!" *Pardon* serves for liberation from sin, the healing of the relationship with God; *peace* serves to heal the wounds of sin, the relationship with oneself and others—and frequently the healing of memories as well.

Conversion, Not Mechanics

This view of confession and its content may seem unfamiliar to many priests and faithful. They will also feel that it is too much to ask that they put such an idea into practice: where will they get the time, not to mention the required knowledge? Besides, there is the force of habit: why should we suddenly reject what has proved itself over so many decades? But we could counter with the question: why are the confessionals increasingly empty at the same time that people are more and more oppressed by guilt feelings? You can see it in their aggression and depression, and often enough in their vehement denial of any form of guilt or sin.

Many people sense instinctively today that their acute problems no longer match the ideas of sin and confession that they learned in the past. Therefore they avoid the confessional and seek their salvation and healing from a guru or a psychiatrist. In fact, most of us are far from being entirely free from a largely mechanical view of sin and penance, as if these were measurable quantities that have practically nothing to do with the mystery of God and God's mercy. It is well known that there were doubts about ordaining the Curé of Ars to the priesthood because he had difficulties with some of the tricky questions on the examination about the sacrament of penance. But that was nearly two hundred years ago. Twenty years ago, when I myself was in the seminary, I had to work my way through a textbook and memorize parts of it. There you could read, literally, that anyone who eats up to sixty grams of liverwurst on Friday has committed a venial sin, but if it was more than sixty grams, it would be a mortal sin. There were other places where you could look up how many "Our Fathers" and "Hail Marys" should be given as penance. So a Catholic only had to set the postal scale on the table at breakfast on Fridays in order to be pretty sure what to expect on Saturday afternoon in the confessional. The relationships were quite clear: it really functioned very smoothly without any reference to God.

The burden of such practices is unfortunately still perceptible today, in that many people continue to think that their sins and forgiveness have more to do with the priest and his attitude of the moment than with God and God's mercy—or, to put it more precisely, with God's *joy* that the lost child has been found again, that it is no longer dead, but living. What does the text say? ". . . while he was yet at a distance, his father saw him and had compassion, and ran and embraced him and kissed him" (Luke 15:20).

Whether confession is again to be a sacrament of reconciliation and healing, and thus a real aid for so many people who are in physical and psychic distress, will depend primarily on the priest's internal attitude toward confession and toward the penitent. For the healing and conversion of the Samaritan woman at Jacob's well, certainly, the humility with which Jesus asked her for a drink of water was more important at the outset than the fact that she was face to face with the Messiah!

How can priests and penitents arrive at an attitude that corresponds to this mutual encounter with the Lord? In the introduction to the ritual of reconciliation it says: "Priest and penitent should first prepare themselves by prayer to celebrate the sacrament. The priest should call upon the Holy Spirit so that he may receive enlightenment and love" (no. 15). And elsewhere:

> In order to fulfill his ministry properly and faithfully the confessor should understand the disorders of souls and apply the appropriate remedies to them. He should fulfill his office of judge wisely and should acquire the knowledge and prudence necessary for this task by serious study, guided by the teaching authority of the Church and especially by fervent prayer to God (no. 10).

Recognizing Evil at the Root

So it is not primarily a question of the priest's technical knowledge, but of prayer, enlightenment, and love—in short, it is a matter of *faith*, which enables him to recognize the soul's sickness and to find the right remedy. Of course, a certain de-

gree of knowledge of the human psyche is a basic precondition of pastoral office. But that certainly does not mean that,
on the basis of such knowledge, sin is to be psychologized out
of existence or rationalized, nor that people should be dis-
couraged from confessing "minor" sins, whereby confession
is made more or less superfluous, as happens all too often
nowadays. To console someone in psychic or spiritual distress
by saying: "That isn't so bad. You do have a problem, but you
can live with it. It's the same for a lot of other people," really
does *not* represent humane understanding, as it is so often and
so proudly called. It is a kind of veiled resignation like that
which exists—explicitly or implicitly—in most psychological
and psychotherapeutic schools. Raising a problem to the conscious level or clarifying it brings neither forgiveness nor healing.[1] A *Christian* healing, in the context of faith in the
redeeming sacrifice of Christ and expecting from him alone the
forgiveness of sins and the consequent healing of the *whole* person, will always recognize the evil at its root and try to get hold
of it there. And that means that the priest will encourage the
penitent to confess the sin they have recognized in their common effort as really *sin*, so that its guilt can be forgiven and
the wound healed. The priest will not say: "That is not so bad.
You can live with it," but instead: "Nothing is so terrible that
it cannot be forgiven by Christ and healed at the root."

Michael Scanlan,[2] the Linn brothers,[3] and Jim McManus[4]
have done substantial preliminary work in this area. McManus
gives the example of a woman, born out of wedlock and diagnosed as chronically depressive, to show that hatred of oneself, one's parents, and God need not poison a whole life and
lead to a definitive picture of illness that looks like severe
depression.[5]

Of course it requires as much courage as humility on the
part of the pastoral minister to explain to a woman diagnosed
by her doctors as a severe depressive that without sorrow and
penance she can obtain neither healing nor reconciliation, because hate is and remains a sin. But the minister should be
aware that any hesitation in confronting the one seeking help

with the real situation of his or her soul could result in making the healing and liberating effect of God's love and mercy unworkable. God will not intervene as long as the human person is not consciously prepared to accept God's help because all human efforts have proved fruitless. But once that readiness has been awakened, God will be able to forgive and heal in the sacrament of reconciliation at a depth that will always remain out of the reach of all human efforts, including the methods of depth psychology. McManus, in describing his procedure in bringing the depressive woman to sorrow over her hatred, refers to the introduction to the new rite of reconciliation:

> For only through *metanoia*, that is, through the transformation of the whole person, is it possible for us to gain access to the kingdom of Christ. In it, we are shaken by the holiness and love of God . . . and begin to reflect, to judge and to put our lives in order. The genuineness of penance depends on this internal sorrow. For conversion must take hold of the person from within in order to lead her or him to deeper insight and to conform him or her more and more to Christ (no. 6).

Social Dimension of Personal Sin

Only this being shaken by the love of God can bring about a transformation of human persons at depth—and thereby cause a reordering and healing of their lives. Without this form of sorrow and penance, which has nothing mechanical or moralizing about it, there can be no healed and renewed relationship with God, with oneself, and with neighbor. It is nothing less than this healing of the whole person, including his or her environment, that is the ultimate goal of the sacrament of reconciliation: "Penance always entails reconciliation with our brothers and sisters who are always harmed by our sins" (no. 5). This touches an essential dimension that has always played a role in the Church's thought but had been completely forgotten in recent years, as consciousness of sin faded: *the social dimension of sin.* In his apostolic exhortation "Reconciliation and Penance,'' December 2, 1984, Pope John Paul II emphasizes that ''there is no sin, not even the most intimate and secret one, the most strictly individual one, that exclusively concerns the person committing it. With greater or lesser violence, with greater or lesser harm, every sin has repercussions on the entire ecclesial body and the whole human family'' (no. 16).

If even a quite personal, intimate sin has a social dimension—secretly hidden, but no less powerful for all that—then public sin against the love of neighbor has an irritating and wounding character for God because it hurts the neighbor and thereby insults the hidden presence of God in her or him. Finally, there is also a social dimension to sin when people in groups injure other groups, for example, through economic injustices within a political system or through brutal exploitation such as that exercised by First World nations against those of the Third World.

Of course, the social dimension of sin never abrogates the personal responsibility of individuals. Even when they are compelled to certain actions as members of a group, or when they act more or less freely in the name of the group, the personal character of their sin is not eliminated.

This declaration of the Pope in his apostolic letter is important because, contrary to an opinion that is widely current, it is never the case that groups or even structures can be sinful. Only persons can sin. Therefore, no one can be freed and healed from sin simply by a change in structures. It is only through the recognition and acknowledgment of their sins and by being forgiven that individuals can become aware that the structures for which they are responsible are evil; and they will only be willing to change them when they *themselves* have changed. The conversion of individuals in sorrow and penance, ''shaken by the love of God,'' will not be without consequence for the fate of the many. If, on the other hand, we insist on the sinfulness of structures and the necessity to change them through merely human efforts, we miss the chance for the conversion and healing of individuals through God's mercy.

Social Dimension of Repentance

The martyrdom of Martin Luther King, Jr. because of his advocacy of nonviolence appears to be a good example of the fact that there is, in the last analysis, no such thing as a sinful situation but only people who let themselves be forced into sinful actions, who can nevertheless be brought by others' example to sorrow and penance and so can be reconciled and healed. Such individuals can then become a blessing for many, even if at first these seem to put no value on that blessing because it can lead them to reflection and finally to conversion as well. "Do what you want with us. Threaten our children, and we will go on loving you. Say that we are low, that we are worthless, and we will go on loving you. Throw bombs into our houses if you want to, and blow up our churches at dawn—we will go on loving you," cried Martin Luther King, Jr. to his oppressors, those who destroyed his house and who finally murdered him. This attitude of consistent nonviolence was to lead to the abolition of many racial laws in America and so to a decisive victory over injustice and oppression.

For Martin Luther King, Jr., this healing of the many through the witness of individuals was unthinkable without the willingness to confess our sins even *to one another*. "Confess your sins to one another, and pray for one another, that you may be healed," as it says in the Letter of James (5:16).

Of course, this confession of sins before the community can only be concerned with sins against the community (and not with intimate sins, even if these cause the community to suffer with the sinner in hidden ways). An open confession of sins in the presence of the community cannot and should not replace individual, private confession and the sacramental absolution that goes with it—just as a communal penance service cannot and should not replace individual confession[6] but instead should lead to it by awakening and sharpening individual consciences to the social dimensions of sin. On the other hand, individual confession neither can nor should in all cases replace the mutual confession of sins within the community.

God can only forgive (in confession) those sins which people have already forgiven one another in sorrow and humility.[7]

The ancient religious orders have received the precious heritage of the "chapter of faults" from their founders. After a period of decline into externals and formalities followed by its complete abolition, the chapter of faults is being recovered in a new form today in many places—simply because it corresponds to a necessity of common life. A community without any form of public confession of sins is wide open to the powers of darkness and confusion. But where people are prepared, through a personal confession in the presence of the brothers and sisters, to let God's light into their own darkness in order that the darkness may be light for all (cf. Eph 5:13), there is room also for salvation, and evil in all its forms must give way. If people are not ready to expose their own poverty and dependence on one another but try instead to maintain the illusion of possible independence, the community would do better not to call itself Christian, because in it the Crucified and Risen One has become illusory, and finally superfluous. The body of Christ is not only sick, but dead in such a place; worse yet, it is nonexistent, because the sign of Christ's life and existence presupposes that each, in humility, values the other more than him- or herself and does not simply look out for her or his own good but for that of the neighbor (cf. Phil 2:3-4). Unless a community and the individuals in it repeatedly and expressly decide for Christ through a confession of sins, they inevitably decide against him: "Whoever is not for me is against me, and whoever does not gather with me, scatters" (Matt 12:30*).

Healing Through Reconciliation: A Personal Story

In conclusion, let me here give a personal witness to the healing of a *whole* person through the sacrament of reconciliation. A student with whom I had traveled abroad some years ago and of whom I had lost nearly all trace in the meantime, suddenly wrote that she wanted to see me. When she arrived, she told me that, after studying linguistics for five years and theology for three more, she had had enough of the West and more than enough of Christianity. She was now going to China on a scholarship to teach languages. So this was a farewell visit. I accepted this announcement without saying much. After two days of insignificant chats she had one of the attacks of cramps under which she had suffered regularly for the past ten years. The doctors had more or less given up and suggested she undertake psychotherapy, because medicine did not seem to help her and the intervals between attacks were getting shorter. Usually the cramps led, within three days, to a total stiffening of her whole body, with severe pain and shortness of breath that approached suffocation and the fear of death that goes with it. Besides all this, the third day of our meeting was the day on which she was supposed to depart, and I also had to leave. Shortly before the high point of the crisis, by which time her movements were those of a drunken person—slow, difficult, and scarcely controllable—she told me about a dream she had had the night before: she had cried out several times in her native language "Lord, have mercy; Christ, have mercy; Lord, have mercy" so loudly that she woke herself up. Still half asleep, she knew she ought to go to confession—something she had not done since the beginning of her theological studies more than three years before. I told her she should not wait any longer. In fact, she pulled out of her pocket a slip of paper on which she had written her sins during the night. The confession, sometimes only in key words, took half an hour. Then we prayed for healing of her relationships, especially to her parents, to the Church, and to priests. Then I gave her absolution—and this woman, who up until that moment had been practically lame, jumped up "and was healed from that hour." Up to today, nearly a year later, she has had no more attacks. In her own humorous way she admitted that some connection between confession, absolution, and physical healing would be hard to deny. For the first time in many years she began to speak again of entering a religious community. "He must really be stronger," she said smilingly. "He caught me out. I don't know how he managed it."

What appears to me central in this healing of the *whole* person through the sacrament of reconciliation is that it was brought about by Jesus, *present in his mystical body*. For the encounter happened within a small, contemplative community where the Liturgy of the Hours and Eucharistic adoration are as important as the constant, personal prayer for each individual guest. What did the Curé of Ars say? "From the beginning of creation to the coming of the Messiah, everything is God's mercy."

Forgiving Oneself and Allowing God to Forgive

I am often asked why sins that have often been confessed and forgiven still return repeatedly to our consciousness. People usually suspect, in such cases, that not everything has been said or that they did not confess precisely enough. Citing the return of the prodigal son (cf. Luke 15:18-21), the Church teaches that the disposition of the penitent to conversion is decisive, not the completeness of the confession. Even sins that have not been named or that have only been generally indicated fall within God's forgiveness, for God knows our hearts. A person who has confessed and received absolution is in the same situation of purification from sin as at the moment of baptism.[8]

If certain sins nevertheless are recalled again later, it is usually because one has let oneself be forgiven by God, but has not forgiven oneself. The word "forgive" means to give something away, to let it loose from one's own hand. If I cling to a consciousness of my sins, even if they have long ago been forgiven by God, I will not be able to get them out of my mind. I have to *believe* that I have been forgiven, and that means concretely that I must separate myself from something that, as far as God is concerned, no longer exists. I cannot expect that God will give me a new heart of flesh and put the divine Spirit within me as long as I am not prepared to surrender my heart of stone (cf. Jer 31:33).⁹

Notes

1. To someone who wanted to get involved in a long discussion of a problem—what many people nowadays call a "thorough discussion in the context of confession"—the Curé of Ars said curtly: "Confession first, discussion afterward." He knew from experience that the grace of confession would make the effort of discussion superfluous.

2. Michael Scanlan and Ann T. Shields, *Their Eyes were Opened*, especially the appendix.

3. Matthew and Dennis Linn, S.J., *Healing Life's Hurts* (New York: Paulist Press, 1978).

4. Jim McManus, *The Healing Power of the Sacraments* (Notre Dame, Ind.: Ave Maria Press, 1984).

5. McManus, pp. 39–42.

6. See the address of John Paul II to the plenary meeting of the Congregation for the Sacraments on 17 April 1986. After the pope had pointed out that general absolution for several persons without previous individual confession is an exception to be used in cases of extreme necessity, he added: "It is the task, therefore, of the pastors to take care, by way of an appropriate catechesis, that no confusion exists in the minds of the faithful between general absolution and individual confession, . . . however, it will be important to help the faithful to discover that it is not merely a matter of obligation [to confess individually] but also of a true and proper *right:* indeed, we find here a reflection of that personal relationship that the Good Shepherd intends to establish with each of his little sheep, whom he knows in a personal way, indeed—according to the beautiful expression of the Gospel of John—whom he 'calls by name' (cf. John 10:3). In the personal conversation with the minister of the sacrament of penance the individual faithful exercises his [her] right to a more personal encounter with Christ crucified, who listens with compassion and forgives; with Christ who says to him [her] again personally with the same words of the Gospel: 'Your sins are forgiven; go, and do not sin again!' (cf. Mark 2:5; John 8:11). By insisting on this aspect of the sacramen-

tal discipline, the Church is safeguarding, basically, the right of the individual to his [her] own unique subjectivity, which cannot be allowed to dissolve into the anonymity of the masses, nor be replaced by the community, however rich and important the contribution of the latter" *(Osservatore Romano,* weekly English edition of 5 May 1986, p. 12).

7. On this point, see the remarks on the Our Father in the previous chapter, "Healing Through the Eucharist."

8. This seems also to be the very clear reason why it is not enough to confess one's sins "directly" to God, something which has become common in many places today, even in the Catholic Church, I regret to say, instead of choosing the way of mediation through the priest and the Church. For only through the authority of the priest in service of the Church can *all* sins be completely forgiven through the sacramental grace of absolution.

9. On this, see the excellent little essay, "Healing the Self-Image Through Personal Prayer," in: Jim McManus, *The Healing Power of the Sacraments,* 101–108.

SEVEN

Healing Through the Sacrament of Orders

"Every priest represents . . . Christ," says Vatican Council II's Decree on the Ministry and Life of Priests. "Therefore, . . . he is also enriched with special grace . . . [so that] the weakness of human flesh can be healed by the holiness of Him who has become for our sake a high priest, 'holy, innocent, undefiled, set apart from sinners' (Heb 7:26)."[1]

So priests also need healing. They, too, can have human weaknesses. The sacrament by which they become priests in the first place will help them both to recognize these weaknesses and to continually overcome them. Here, too, it is a question of a process: "By the sacrament of orders priests are configured to Christ the Priest," says the decree.[2] Certainly this "configuration" is not to be understood as an identity but rather as an ideal, or, more precisely, a promise. Christ knows that priests, in their human weakness, will need a continual renewal of special grace—that is, constant healing—in order that they may *become* configured to him.

What are the characteristics of this healing? How does the priest actually obtain it? Through *service* to the community. The sentence already quoted above: "By the sacrament of orders priests are configured to Christ the Priest," continues and is given its rationale in these words: "so that as ministers of the Head and co-workers of the episcopal order they can build up

and establish His whole body which is the Church.''[3] It also
says: ''. . . by their everyday sacred actions themselves, as
by the entire ministry. . . they are being directed toward perfection of life.'' So priests are very concretely said to be being
healed of their human weaknesses, even to the point of configuration to Christ, in the exercise of their ministry—and in
the awareness that this ministry is always a service to the
people of God, to the *body of Christ*. For it is only through the
holiness of Christ and of his body that priests can experience
their own sanctification and healing. It follows that the ministry of priests in the Church and for the Church must be experienced and exercised primarily as a *sacramental* ministry, if
it is going to heal and sanctify the priest. For ''the church is
a kind of sacrament of intimate union with God, and of the
unity of all [hu]mankind, that is, she is a sign and an instrument of such union and unity.''[4]

Strictly speaking, this sacramental ministry of priests, which
contributes to their healing and sanctification, is a *Eucharistic*
ministry. Cardinal Ratzinger calls the Church's self-under-
standing as presented by Vatican Council II a ''Eucharistic ec-
clesiology'': ''Jesus's last supper is recognized as the true act
of the founding of the Church. Jesus bestows the liturgy of
his death and resurrection on those who are his and thus
bestows on them the feast of life. . . . For that reason the
Church Fathers could say so beautifully that the Church sprang
from the opened side of the Lord, out of which flowed both
blood and water.''[5]

Healing Self and Others

Priests, then, will be healed when, in the encounter with
the community as body of Christ, they again and again receive
this gift of the ''feast of life'' which the Eucharist really is—
and, of course, the other sacraments as well. They will be made
whole by joining with Jesus in surrendering their life, the gift
of God the Father, ''out of love for their friends.'' As the Council says: ''they are grounded in the life of the Spirit while they

exercise the ministry of the Spirit and of justice (cf. 2 Cor 3:8-9), as long as they are docile to Christ's Spirit, who vivifies and leads them.''[6]

This Spirit of Christ should not only form and shape the ministry of priests to the body of Christ, but their entire lives as well. Priests' healing happens when they allow themselves to be vivified and led by this Spirit of Christ, the Spirit of the Savior, and by no other spirit. That sounds obvious. And yet for many, especially older priests, it is not as clear as the Council makes it sound. Here the "destruction of the works of the flesh" does not come about in the first place through one's own effort, that is, through ascetic "exercises" and self-denial, but instead through the "anointing of the Holy Spirit" and the mission given by Christ.[7] So priests do not owe their devotion to any works done for their own sake; instead, they receive it through their anointing and sending by the Spirit of God, a mission that becomes concrete in the performance of the sacred actions, that is, the administration of the sacraments and every other ministry done for the people of God as body of Christ.

Thus, priests do not owe their healing and sanctification in the first place to their own activities. Instead, they receive them mainly as a gift. And they need these gifts so that their ministry will bear fruit. "Priestly holiness . . . contributes very greatly to a fruitful fulfillment of the priestly ministry.''[8] This fruitfulness, of course, does not refer to any statistically measurable success that might result from the priest's capability. That kind of success usually happens at the expense of the spiritual fruitfulness of the priestly ministry—and thereby often at the expense of the priest's spiritual and physical health—because it causes the priest to look to other "gods" and not to Jesus Christ and accustoms the faithful also to seek values other than faith in Jesus. Certainly a varied program exercises a certain attraction. Productivity always excites a lot of interest in what can be done. But it also leads to a competitive ideal and thus to tensions and divisions instead of to unity and love within the one body of Christ.

In Unity with Christ

What medicines does the sacrament of orders provide in the daily life of priests? The conciliar decree (after the "sacred actions," that is, the administration of the sacraments) mentions in the first place daily contact with the sacred Scriptures, and this again as an opportunity for personal encounter with Jesus:

> Since they are ministers of God's Word, they should every day read and listen to that Word which they are required to teach to others. . . . Remembering that it is the Lord who opens hearts (cf. Acts 16:14) and that sublime utterance comes not from themselves but from God's power (cf. 2 Cor 4:7), in the very act of preaching His word they will be united more closely with Christ the Teacher and be led by His Spirit. Thus joined to Christ, they will share in God's love. . . .[9]

The healing effect of dealing with sacred Scripture thus flows from *experiencing* the Word as a personal relationship with Jesus who reveals to us the Father's love. Without this personal encounter and the experience of God's love, the only way in which the meaning of Scripture can be opened to us, daily Bible reading can become routine and its content will appear to us to be abstract rather than healing, naive rather than reconciling.

In Unity with the Church

The same kind of healing and reconciling effect should result from the priest's daily prayer of the Liturgy of the Hours: "By reciting the Divine Office, they lend their voice to the Church as in the name of all humanity she perseveres in prayer along with Christ, who 'lives always to make intercession for us' (Heb 7:25)."[10] Here, too, healing occurs through the priest's unity with Christ, the Savior, and through service to the Church as Christ's body. Praying the breviary is a work of reconciliation and thus of healing, even when the priest prays it alone, because through this prayer a priest is continually united with the whole Church in heaven and on earth and prays for the peace of *all* humankind. The Liturgy of the Hours is an effective means to bring peace and reconciliation in situations in which all other methods have failed and when it seems there can be no hope of success.

The conciliar decree also says of priests: ''They give to their people signs of unshakeable hope.''[11] This hope for the coming reign of God and ultimately for the return of Christ seems to me to be one of the indispensable means of healing in the life of priests and their congregations. In their frustration at the lack of visible results, it is easy for priests to lapse into resignation, which can take a wide variety of forms: flight into exaggerated activity, into human contacts that are more and more superficial, into excessive intellectual activity—or even psychic and physical illness. An especially dangerous form of resignation, negatively understood and one we already mentioned in the previous chapter on the sacrament of reconciliation, seems to be the inclination to try to explain everything psychologically or sociologically. The twofold ''advantage,'' which is basically nothing but illusion, seems to be, in the first place, the creation of a distance between the person of the priest, the community, the superior, the Church, and the mystery of God; more precisely, it consists of keeping people and things at a distance, where they threaten to touch and wound us. The second advantage is that, in creating this distance, we think we have found a means for keeping an oversight on things, having a hold on people and things, or, more precisely, controlling them and not being controlled by them. Of course, such an attitude leads to isolation—and the less we are aware of it, the more intense is the effect. Thereby it draws us into still further frustration and resignation. A priest can seem impressively productive, but the work will not bear the least spiritual fruit. It will have no healing effect, either for the priest or for anyone else.

Therefore it is very wise of the Church to remind priests to be in themselves signs of unshakeable hope for the faithful, namely, out of that inner, secure consciousness of their unity with Christ, of which Paul could say: "Our hope for you is unshaken; for we know that as you share in our sufferings, you will also share in our comfort" (2 Cor 1:7).

This comfort, in the mind of the apostle and of Vatican Council II, does not consist solely in unity with Christ but also in unity with the whole Church. To avoid the dangers of distraction, even to the point of inner strife, priests should "unit[e] themselves with Christ in acknowledging the Father's will [cf. John 4:34]"[12] and exercise their ministry "by hierarchical communion with the whole body."[13] The Council also tells us what the healing effect of this unity is: "This obedience leads to the more mature freedom of God's [children]."[14]

Healing Through Celibacy

In this personal union with Christ and his Church, in the comfort the priest derives from them, we also find the healing and reconciling basis for celibacy. Remaining unmarried should not imply a renunciation on the part of the priest, but on the contrary, it represents the offer of the greater freedom of the children of God. It should enable the priest more easily "to hold fast to [Christ] with an undivided heart" (cf. 1 Cor 7:32-34)[15] and to be "all things to all." Thus, celibacy can never be seen or lived as a static situation. It is a gift of grace, ever renewed, and ever to be asked for anew. Celibacy is not a state, and therefore the difficulties that everyone has with it sooner or later are not incurable. Like every relationship, including marriage, celibacy also requires development. Depending on their age and situation, priests will find themselves in new and different phases of celibacy—and thereby they will experience the richness and variety of this gift of grace. The opinion of many psychological schools, namely, that celibacy is contrary to human nature because humans are directed to an active sexual life, confirms that it is a *grace* of unity with Christ, and that celibacy must be lived as a *gift* in a well-balanced way. Therefore the attempt to give a *merely* psychological or sociological explanation of celibacy and its corresponding way of life is not only dangerous but extremely misguided and even fatal. Such an explanation will inevitably lead to an imbalance, with all its destructive consequences and compensations. But the cause of such an imbalance is not celibacy itself; it is a fundamentally false attitude toward this *gift*, no matter how solid the scientific basis for such an attitude may seem.

For in the last analysis, celibacy can only be understood and lived out of faith. And only on the basis of faith can it also contribute to the healing of the whole priest and the whole Church. Thus the priest's healing through celibacy will also depend essentially on whether he sees the Church as merely a sociological phenomenon—the people of God, let us say—or as a sacramental reality: more precisely, as a Eucharistic reality, namely, the body of Christ, born from the surrender of that body out of love for his friends (cf. John 15:13).

Because priests must always be concerned for the whole Church as the one body of Christ, the Council says explicitly that they should have personal associates with whom they have "friendly and fraternal dealings."[16] But these nuanced relationships with others, which are absolutely indispensable, can only contribute to priests' psychic balance if they always remain aware that, although living in the world, they do not belong to the world (cf. John 17:14-16). To speak more clearly, a priest's friendship conflicts with his calling when he desires to *have* a man or a woman exclusively for himself and his needs: when he no longer experiences the other as a gift that may be taken away from him, or that he may have to renounce freely if he notices that there is a monopolizing claim on one side or the other. Priests can only be healers, and themselves the recipients of undivided wholeness and salvation, if it is clear to everyone that they are called first and last to serve the *whole* Church and *everyone*—and that they are responsible to God for their call.

An essential aid to priests in living their celibacy in a healthy fashion is therefore prayer to Mary, especially the Rosary. By her unconditioned and unrestricted yes to the will of God in every situation—from the annunciation to the crucifixion—

Mary is the one who knew better than anyone how to renounce her own will in the most interior fashion, and who saw in doing the will of her Son a promise that was constantly renewed. Her life did not thereby become impoverished or neglected; instead, she experienced a constant enrichment and fulfillment. Therefore, especially for the sake of a wholesome recollection at moments of inner strife and as a relief of tension in times when one is overstretched, the contemplation of the mysteries of God in the Rosary is an indispensable aid to priests in keeping their balance. The same can be said, obviously, for short visits to the Lord in the tabernacle and even more for Eucharistic adoration.

Among the most valuable experiences of my priestly life, I count those healings of body and soul that came about solely through the encounter with the Lord in Eucharistic adoration, after all other medical and psychological efforts had been fruitless.

Notes

1. Decree on the Ministry and Life of Priests, 12.

2. *Ibid.*

3. *Ibid.*

4. *LG* 1.

5. *Communio (International Catholic Review)* 13, 3 (Fall 1986), p. 242.

6. Decree on the Ministry and Life of Priests, 12.

7. *Ibid.*

8. *Ibid.*

9. *Ibid.*, 13.

10. *Ibid.*

11. *Ibid.*

12. *Ibid.*, 14.

13. *Ibid.*, 15.

14. *Ibid.*

15. *Ibid.*, 16.

16. *Ibid.*, 17.

EIGHT

Healing Through the Sacrament of Marriage

"**Y**ou did not choose me, but I chose you and appointed you that you should go and bear fruit and that your fruit should abide. . . . This I command you, to love one another" (John 15:16-17). What was said of healing through the sacrament of orders is true in a corresponding fashion of healing through the sacrament of marriage: each sacrament brings healing simply because it is a gift of the Savior, even though each presupposes, as a matter of course, our readiness to be led and healed by him. But the initiative *always* comes from him, even if we often find it difficult to recognize and acknowledge it.

According to the view of the Old Testament, marriage is an image of the loving relationship between God and God's people. In the eyes of the early Church it is an image of the covenant between Christ and the Church as his mystical body (cf. Eph 5:25-32). So it is not that God chose the union between two human persons as an exemplary image for the covenant between God and God's people, as is often said, but instead, we human beings are capable of joining in a covenant with one another only because God has given us an example of such a union and continues to give us that example—and because the initiative for the covenant proceeds from God, and it is God who continually affirms and gives life to that covenant. This tells us already that the sacrament of marriage is not exhausted in a single incident, that is, in the wedding celebration. From this sacrament as from every other proceeds a healing and healthful process that lasts, or should last, for a lifetime.

For in addition to the partners' readiness to accept and cooperate with the initiative of God and the Holy Spirit—to the extent that their yes to one another is like Mary's yes to the angel's message at the moment of the annunciation—marriage also includes the constant openness of both partners to allowing themselves to be touched, healed, and even transformed by the healing effects of the grace of the sacrament.

A special mystery of *marriage* as a covenant initiated by God is that it is the *partners* who constantly and repeatedly bestow divine grace on each other. Vatican Council II says that marriage finds its meaning in the spouses' being "witnesses to one another . . . of faith in Christ and love for Him."[1] Living a married life through the grace of the sacrament thus implies a healing process resting on mutuality and communion: the partners experience healing together in the faith that God has united them and continues to sustain their union; they experience mutual healing as they continue to give to one another and receive from one another, in mutual trust, the graces they have received from God.

Biblical Character of Marriage

The healing effect of such a marriage for the world surrounding it lies in the fact that the relationship of the partners to one another and to God witnesses to the reality of the reign of God in this world. The Council gives special emphasis to this aspect: "The Christian family loudly proclaims . . . the present virtues of the kingdom of God. . . ."[2] This should occur through a continual healing from every form of individualism, for "just as [Christ] loved the Church and handed Himself over on her behalf, the spouses [are to] love each other with perpetual fidelity through mutual self-bestowal."[3]

This may all appear quite idealistic and unrealistic, since it is so different from what we are used to and what we see around us. But we can scarcely expect that Christ will adapt his gospel to our expectations so that it may appear realistic. Nor can we ask the Church to shape its idea of marriage, which rests essentially on the gospel, more in accord with what is "really our lived experience" today, rather than with what God has revealed to the Church through the gospel. We could ask more concretely: how can we expect healing from marriage as long as we call "realistic" the things that are totally strange to the gospel, and consider the reality that Jesus lived to be idealistic?

In pastoral practice I am continually appalled to see how many young couples speak quite as a matter of course of their readiness to enter into Christian marriage, while in fact they are not at all prepared for mutual service. Instead, their attitude is purely one of secular consumerism: everything, including their sexual relationship, is evaluated in terms of how much the other "brings" me and how much I need to "invest" in order for it to be "worthwhile." It is scarcely astonishing that such marriages are deeply marked by a fear of being taken advantage of, or even of being "fired" when one or the other is no longer adequate to satisfy the other partner's demands and needs. The first destructive aspect of this attitude toward marriage is the radical commercialization of every human relationship, which means concretely the unavoidable reaching for power that can lead to nothing but egocentricity and isolation, which are the opposites of any and all fruitfulness.

Still more destructive than this idea of marriage, which in itself is already totally unbiblical, is the confusion experienced by many Christian married couples resulting from the fact that many Christian institutions, including parishes and counseling services, while they preach what the Church teaches really work on the basis of psychological findings that, under such designations as "self-realization" and "adulthood," represent the exact opposite of the Church's teaching—not to mention the inclination of many pastors and pastoral ministers toward "intensifying" marriage through charlatan versions of Eastern religions. In this most regrettable lumping together of

Church teaching and unbiblical practice, many must really get the impression that the Church, on the one hand, clings to "outmoded" ideas like "continence" and "marital discipline" and, on the other hand, propagates practices that are based on a purely materialistic image of human persons, their needs, and the ways of satisfying those needs.

Dignity of the Body

It is true that this confusion may be explained in large part by the heavy burden of that supposedly Christian hatred of the body from which the Church, in its preaching and practice, is far from being healed. Let me say here once more with the greatest possible clarity what ought to have been self-evident to all Christians for a long time: according to the Bible, both in the Old and New Testaments, Christianity is in no way to be understood as the enemy of the body. On the contrary: through the divine incarnation and Christ's bodily resurrection from the dead, the human body—more precisely, the human person in his/her body—has received a dignity and coresponsibility for creation that is not present in any other religion or culture. "Glorify God in your body," says the apostle Paul. Just before this he had written: "God raised the Lord and will also raise us up by his power. Do you not know that your bodies are members of Christ? . . . Do you not know that your body is a temple of the Holy Spirit within you, which you have from God? You are not your own; you were bought with a price. So glorify God in your body" (1 Cor 6:14-20). So despising the body is neither biblical nor Christian. It crept into the Christian tradition through Greek philosophy, specifically Neoplatonism, for which the body was a prison for the soul and the soul's whole effort must be to free itself from this slavery. For centuries this idea dominated the Church's teaching, though it was never totally victorious—one need only read some of the medieval or baroque wedding sermons to see the freedom with which our forebears in faith could speak, within the liturgy, about the ways of the body! Or take the attitude of a saint and teacher of the Church like Thomas Aquinas toward the body: "O boundless giver, lend to my body the beauty of transparency, facility of penetration, delicacy of feeling and the power of immortality."

It may be that the address of this prayer, "O boundless giver," is strange to us and therefore not immediately comprehensible. The same may be said of the final petition, for "the power of immortality." Our attitude toward the body and thus also to marriage and its consummation will only contribute to our life's fulfillment when we regard ourselves and other people not as possessions at our disposal, but always and ever anew as a gift, and that means as completely undeserved gift, for which we can only render astonished thanks. The natural result of such an attitude will be respect for one's own bodily life and that of the other. Nor can we earn for ourselves the power of immortality. It is given to us through our redemption to everlasting life, and therefore solely through the sacrifice of Christ.

Cocreators with God

Both elements—our body as undeserved gift and its redemption to eternal life—are decisive for a Christian understanding of our own physical being and of our relationship to our marriage partner. Without this basic attitude, in which the whole dignity and coresponsibility of the human being as made in the image of the Creator is reflected, and therefore also the human being as cocreator with God, there would be no sense in saying of married couples that their willingness to serve and their fidelity are witnesses to the service and fidelity of God. The indissolubility of Christian marriage has its deepest roots in this fidelity of God to creatures. To question it would be to doubt *God's* fidelity—and that can only lead to despair. Certainly, when married couples are not prepared to serve one another and to remain faithful, they not only bring God's fidelity into question, but also the fulfillment of their relationship in mutual surrender. "The total physical self-giving would be a lie if it were not the sign and fruit of a total personal self-giving, in which the whole person, including the temporal dimension, is present. If the person were to withhold something or reserve the possibility of deciding otherwise in the future, by this very fact he or she would not be giving totally."[4]

The Church's affirmation of human beings, their bodiliness, their sexuality, and their capability of self-surrender goes still further: through their mutual sexual surrender and fruitfulness, married couples witness to God's creative power; in fact, they themselves cooperate in the divine creative power: "[Parents] should realize that they are . . . cooperators with the love of God the Creator, and are, so to speak, the interpreters of that love."[5] John Paul II takes up this conciliar text and expands it in light of the special fecundity of human beings and its meaning:

> With the creation of man and woman in his own image and likeness, God crowns and brings to perfection the work of his hands: He calls them to a special sharing in his love and in his power as creator and Father through their free and responsible cooperation in transmitting the gift of human life: "God blessed them, and God said to them: Be fruitful and multiply, and fill the earth and subdue it" (Gen 1:28).[6]

It is only in this union of human self-surrender and fecundity that human beings can grow entirely beyond themselves, rise above all egocentric temptations toward an exclusive concentration on pleasure, and so grow into the image of the Creator. Still more: they overcome the temporal limitations placed on their earthly lives by original sin and gain a share in redemption to eternal life through the very fact that they become co-creators of new life. The Council expressly underlines this function of human sexuality and fertility: it is a question of human coresponsibility not only for God's creation but also for salvation to eternal life: ". . . human life and the task of transmitting it are not realities bound up with this world alone . . . but always have a bearing on the eternal destiny of [human beings]."[7]

And with this we come to the particular healing function of the sacrament of marriage and its consummation: through their fidelity and fertility—both spiritual and physical—the partners grow in their total self-surrender beyond every form of limitation in their lives and become sharers in eternal life. The Council goes so far as to speak not only of healing through the sacrament of marriage but even of a sanctification of the married couple through its consummation: ''. . . by the joys and sacrifices of their vocation and through their faithful love, married people will become witnesses of the mystery of that love which the Lord revealed to the world by His dying and His rising up to life again.''[8]

Through this total consummation of the relationship between the partners as an unearned gift from God to one another, *in addition to* and as an expression of salvation to eternal life, still other limitations and disturbances will be alleviated, such as a lack of mutual understanding or even psychic and physical ailments of one partner or the other.

I myself experienced how a husband's trust in God's help brought his wife, the mother of four small children, to prayer. She was suffering from cancer of the uterus and was about to undergo radical surgery. Her prayer made the operation unnecessary. The surgeons found no symptoms in the woman afterward. This mutual experience not only renewed their marriage but also caused both partners to turn anew to the Bible and the Church.[9]

Notes

1. *LG* 35.

2. *Ibid.*

3. Vatican Council II, Constitution on the Church in the Modern World *(Gaudium et Spes,* hereafter abbreviated *GS*) 48.

4. John Paul II, Apostolic Exhortation, *Familiaris Consortio. On the Duties of the Christian Family in the World Today,* Nov. 22, 1985, no. 11.

5. *GS* 50.

6. *Familiaris Consortio*, no. 28.

7. *GS* 51.

8. *Ibid.*, 52.

9. The much-discussed questions of extramarital relationships, artificial birth control, abortion, and the pastoral care of divorced and remarried people are not considered here, because they are not directly related to the subject of *healing* through the sacrament of *marriage*. Readers may turn in this connection to the especially sensitive book by Jean Vanier, *Community and Growth: Our Pilgrimage Together* (New York: Paulist Press, 1979).

NINE

Healing Through the Sacrament of Anointing

The healing of the sick is a central focus of the New Testament. Jesus does not reserve his authority over this duty given him by his Father, but shares it with his disciples and with all who believe in him. In the Gospel of Luke he says to the disciples: ''Whenever you enter a town . . . heal the sick in it and say to them, 'The kingdom of God has come near to you' '' (10:8-9). In the longer ending of the Gospel of Mark this assignment is extended even further: ''And these signs will accompany those who believe: . . . they will lay their hands on the sick, and they will recover'' (16:17-18). The mandate here contains not only authority but also promise, and it is not just for a chosen few, such as the disciples or the saints, but for *all* who believe. Healing the sick is therefore a mandate given by the Lord to the whole Church, and thus it is a service of every Christian for the body of Christ.

That is why it also says in the Letter of James:

> Are any among you sick? Let them call for the elders of the church, and let them pray over them, anointing them with oil in the name of the Lord; and the prayer of faith will save those who are sick, and the Lord will raise them up; and if they have committed sins, they will be forgiven. Therefore confess your sins to one another, and pray for one another, that you may be healed (5:15-16).

95

This text is considered to represent the earliest form of the
sacrament of healing the sick. Others have discussed how it
could have happened that this sacrament was increasingly
robbed of its original purpose of strengthening and healing and
came to be known, right into our own time, as the "last anointing."[1] In the present time it continues to be connected more
with death than with life in the minds of many: when, in the
place of the doctor in a white smock, the priest in a black cas-
sock appears, things are "serious," and the chances of survival are practically zero.

So it does not seem superfluous even in our own time to
discuss the subject of *healing* through the sacrament of anointing of the sick. Vatican Council II certainly made an effort to
reemphasize the original meaning of this sacrament, but experience shows that quite some time elapses before a conciliar text
becomes part of general Christian consciousness—especially
when customary attitudes on the subject already exist, be these
biblically founded or not.

What is the purpose of the renewed sacrament of anointing of the sick? What is to be healed, and how? In the introduction to the new rite it says:

> This sacrament gives the grace of the Holy Spirit to those who
> are sick: by this grace the whole person is helped and saved
> sustained by trust in God, and strengthened against the temp-
> tations of the Evil One and against anxiety over death. Thus
> the sick person is able not only to bear suffering bravely, but
> also to fight against it. A return to physical health may follow
> the reception of the sacrament if it will be beneficial to the sick
> person's salvation. If necessary, the sacrament also provides
> the person with the forgiveness of sins, and the completion of
> Christian penance (no. 6).

Healing of the Whole Person

This text, promulgated in 1969 as a result of the postcon-
ciliar liturgical reforms, recovers all the essential elements that
we find in James 5. It is a matter *neither* exclusively of human

spiritual welfare *nor* solely of physical healing; it concerns the healing of the whole person, in body *and* soul *and* spirit—in the last analysis, it is a matter of the restoration of the unity of the whole person to the extent that this unity has been disturbed in one area or another.

This restoration of the whole person in his or her original unity and harmony is the work of the Holy Spirit, as we hear. But to make possible this effect of the Holy Spirit, it presupposes the sick person's confession of sins, sorrow, and penance, so that God can forgive these sins and heal the sick person. That is, openness on the part of the human person is a precondition. It is important to know this in celebrating the sacrament. Whether it takes place in the sick person's house, in connection with a liturgical celebration—for example, a Eucharistic liturgy in a church—or at some other Christian celebration, the sick person or persons and the people in their immediate family and neighborhood should prepare themselves thoroughly in prayer, so as to open themselves to the Holy Spirit. The sick person should never be left alone when the sacrament is celebrated. Whether at home or in a large community celebration, the sick should be surrounded by relatives or friends who celebrate with them and pray for their healing, because this prayer receives its effectiveness through the community of the faithful as a cell of the body of Christ. Besides, the sickness of *one* member usually causes a crisis for the whole family, who thus need healing also.

However, one should under no circumstances neglect the offer of a private confession of sins to the priest. When, for practical reasons, that is not possible, the Liturgy of the Word should be introduced by a penitential rite in which each person can publicly acknowledge her or his sins against the neighbor. Often a sick person, before receiving the sacrament, has an intense *need* to confess guilt or be reconciled—and it is extremely important to pay attention to this desire to "make a clean slate."

The texts for the Liturgy of the Word and the priest's or deacon's homily should emphasize the central mandate of *Jesus* to heal the sick and encourage the *faith* of the sick person in God's healing love. In all this, the healing of the *whole* person should be clearly in focus: without a conversion to Jesus, without a personal encounter with him as the Savior, there can be no alleviation of physical symptoms—or at least the true meaning of such relief has not become evident. McManus also tells of the healing of psychic illnesses, such as anxiety, depression, and inability to trust, through the celebration of this sacrament.[2] Often these and similar psychic disturbances hide behind physical symptoms, and the latter cannot be healed over the long term without doing something about the former. Therefore it is important in every case to pray for the healing of the *whole* person and to say so plainly. It may be noted in addition that this total healing is the subject of the prayers in the new rite. First, at the blessing of oil, we have: "Through your blessing let it be for all who are anointed with it a blessed oil, a holy sign of your mercy that drives out sickness, pain and care, a protection for body, soul and spirit" (no. 75). During the anointing the priest prays: "Through this holy anointing may the Lord in his love and mercy help you with the grace of the Holy Spirit. May the Lord who frees you from sin save you and raise you up" (no. 25). And the prayer after the anointing says: "Lord Jesus Christ, our Redeemer, by the grace of your Holy Spirit cure the weakness of your servant. Heal his/her sickness and forgive his/her sins; expel all afflictions of mind and body; mercifully restore him/her to full health, and enable him/her to resume his/her former duties, for you are Lord for ever and ever" (no. 125).

Reintegration into the Community

Another thing that is important in celebrating this sacrament is the reintegration of the sick person in his or her family or community. Sick people often feel helpless and useless—and thus vulnerable and excluded, even and especially when they are particularly well cared for and tended. They do not want to be the "objects" of excessive attention.

They need friends, not caregivers. They need to know that they are not just receivers but also have something to give. Whenever possible they should be allowed to join actively in the prayers; not only formulating spontaneous prayers out loud, but while or after hands are laid on them, they should also lay their hands on the others and so be a blessing to them as they are to the sick ones. Just this mutual laying-on of hands can become a strong element of integration, which often has a stronger effect on those with psychic illnesses than on those who are physically ill. But it is certainly not a "dogma." There may be a variety of reasons why sick (or well) people would *not* want to lay hands on one another. They should never be forced to it, and they should be asked in advance whether they really want to do it.

Openness, Not Expectations

As the celebration of the sacrament should be marked by a great degree of receptivity to the suggestions of the Spirit and the needs of the sick person or persons and their family or community, so also all those who take part should be very open in their expectations regarding the "results" or fruits of this celebration. Too much fixation on the relief of particular symptoms, which may not occur immediately or ever, can easily awaken feelings of guilt on the part of the sick persons and also on the part of their family and friends, with the idea that one didn't pray "properly": not intensively enough or not with the right attitude—or even that they were not worthy of the desired healing. The decisive elements are receptiveness and trust that God *always* wants to heal *everyone*—but that we have to be just as open to the *way* in which God, in loving and penetrating knowledge of every individual and his or her needs, wants to heal here and now.

So if, after the celebration of the sacrament, the healing prayed for does not immediately occur as desired, that is by no means a signal for discouragement. There are many reasons why a person is not healed or not right away or not in the way expected.[3]

One common reason is that healing takes time (especially in chronic illnesses), and thus the celebration of the sacrament should be repeated as often as necessary until a breakthrough toward a definitive healing makes its appearance. If that does not happen *solely* through celebration of the sacrament of anointing, it seems appropriate to combine it with the celebration of other sacraments. I have already mentioned the combined celebration of anointing with the sacrament of reconciliation or with the Eucharist. This should always be done with attention to the Church's texts and instructions. The nature of the celebration should be such that neither the sick persons nor their family and friends have the feeling of being isolated; on the contrary, they should feel themselves integrated in the Church's community life. And this community as well, the local parish, for example, should not treat the sick as something special or unusual, but as people who need salvation and healing like everyone else. Therefore the celebration of anointing of the sick in connection with the Sunday community Eucharist is especially rich in blessing for everyone, because here the whole body of Christ is gathered to be healed and united through the power of the Holy Spirit.

Notes

1. See, for example, Francis McNutt, *The Power to Heal* (Notre Dame, Ind.: Ave Maria Press, 1977), pp. 190ff.

2. On this, see Jim McManus, *The Healing Power of the Sacraments*, 58–61.

3. See F. McNutt, *The Power to Heal*, "Eleven Reasons Why People Are Not Healed," and Michael Marsch, *Heilen* (Salzburg, 1983), "Der Stachel im Fleisch. Warum Menschen nicht geheilt werden [The Thorn in the Flesh. Why People Are Not Healed]."

TEN

Healing Through Mary
and the Communion of Saints

The Instruction from the Congregation for the Doctrine of the Faith of March 22, 1986, "On Christian Freedom and Liberation," says of the healing of the whole Church through Mary's example:

> It is really in the light of faith that one comes to understand how salvation history is the history of liberation from evil in its most radical form and of the introduction of humanity into the true freedom of the children of God. Mary is totally dependent on her Son and completely directed towards him by the impulse of her faith; and, at his side, she is the most perfect image of freedom and of the liberation of humanity and of the universe. It is to her as Mother and Model that the Church must look in order to understand in its completeness the meaning of her own mission (no. 97).

Healing and liberation are a unity for Christians. Healing finally means nothing else but liberation from evil. All the powers of sickness, destruction, and death are outgrowths of evil, visible signs of its invisible power. Mary, as the mother of Jesus, is the one through whom salvation became human. Therefore she is an example and image for us of what healing and liberation can do. As the one who trod on the head of the serpent (cf. Rev 12) and as mother of the Church she herself is a "sacrament," that is, "[a sign and an instrument] of inti-

mate union with God, and of the unity of all [hu]man-
kind. . . .''[1]

Mary's importance as a sign and instrument of unity, freedom, salvation, and healing for the whole Church—all this precisely through her "most intimate union with God"—is
especially impressive if we read and interpret Vatican II's Dogmatic Constitution on the Church in light of its conclusion,
which is the crown of the whole: I mean on the basis of chapter eight on Mary and chapter seven on the communion of
saints. Concerning Mary as model and mother of the Church,
the Council does *not* say, in the first place, that she is *above*
all creatures, but instead, in the words of the document: "she
stands out among the poor and humble of the Lord." Only
afterward is she described as the "exalted Daughter of Sion."[2]
Thus the Church's service can only be a healing service and
have a healing function for the Church itself if it is really a service exercised in humility and poverty. Even more than through
her obedience in faith, Mary is enabled to exercise her service
in poverty because of her *trust* in God. This trust of Mary's
extends from the angel's announcement to her Son's cross.
Only through her unconditioned trust is she able to become
coredemptrix with her Son, and so to be a saving healer along-
side Jesus, the Savior.

Mary, the Vessel of Grace

Mary shows the way for the Church: healing means remaining near, being helpful, while always being conscious of one's
own poverty and total dependence on others and on the Savior. It was from this consciousness of dependence that Mary
grew worthy to be both the mother of the Church and the "exalted Daughter of Sion." Mary, like Jesus, is one of the people
of Israel; she belongs to them in being "God's first love." She
is "beautiful" and "exalted," not for her own sake, but
through Jesus and her humble love for him. She lets herself
be marked by his wounds, and "through his wounds we are
healed" (cf. Isa 53). So it is not so much through active effort

on behalf of the poor but more importantly by knowing itself to be one of the poor that the Church can do a saving and healing work, together with Jesus and in the image of Mary. For the Church can only heal to the extent that it knows itself to be radically dependent on the authority of the Savior to free human beings from the power of evil by delivering them from all sin.

Referring to the early Fathers of the Church, the Council says of Mary that she is "holy and free from all stain of sin."[3] This freedom from sin, that is, her unstained purity and holiness, can only be explained through her poverty: she was conceived completely free of original sin in order to be totally and exclusively the *vessel* of the grace of her Lord. It is true that the angel of the Lord greets her as "full of grace," but she understands herself as a witness to her own poverty when she answers: "Behold, I am the handmaid of the Lord; let it be done to me according to your word." So also she comments on this statement later in her Magnificat: "The Lord has done great things for me; he has regarded the low estate of his handmaiden."

It is precisely because of her attitude of total openness in faith that, in the opinion of the early Fathers of the Church, Mary has a share in the salvation and healing of humanity. In this connection the Council cites Irenaeus of Lyons, a second-century Church Father: "being obedient, [she] became the cause of salvation for herself and for the whole human race."[4]

St. Jerome, in the fourth century, goes a step further: "death through Eve, life through Mary."[5] The very clear conclusion is: all evil came into the world through Eve's disobedience, through the temptation to self-glorification; all good and all life come through Mary's faithful obedience. Her loving trust extends even to the death of her Son on the cross: she "loyally persevered in her union with her Son unto the cross. There she stood, in keeping with the divine plan (cf. John 19:25), suffering grievously with her only-begotten Son. There she united herself with a maternal heart to His sacrifice, and lovingly consented to the immolation of this Victim which she herself had brought forth.''[6] It is just in this loving consent to the death of her Son, that is, in her genuine suffering together with Jesus, that Mary shows her coredeeming *presence for us:* her healing and protecting strength in the midst of the greatest abandonment and insecurity—and it is in this way that she becomes the mother of the Church. ''Finally, the same Christ Jesus dying on the cross gave her as a mother to His disciple. This He did when He said: 'Woman, behold thy son' (John 19:26-27).''[7]

Mary, the Model of Submission

This coredeeming presence based on trusting and loving obedience in faith is the source also of Mary's purity and her continual submission. ''Do whatever he tells you,'' she says at the marriage feast in Cana (John 2:5). The Council lays great value on this submission of Mary's, probably to counter any absolutizing of Marian devotion and so to take into account a justified Protestant criticism of certain excessive forms of Catholic piety. Mary is certainly ''mother to us in the order of grace,'' the Council says,[8] but it insists that ''there is only *one* God and *one* mediator between God and humanity, . . . who gave himself a ransom for all (cf. 1 Tim 2:5-6).''[9] Mary, and reverence for her in the Church, can thus in no way claim to put Jesus in the shade or even to be equal to him. The Council emphasizes that ''all the saving influences of the Blessed Virgin on [human beings] originate . . . from the superabundance of the merits of Christ, rest on his mediation, depend entirely on it, and draw all their power from it.''[10] Nor do the various titles of honor given to Mary, most of which go back to the earliest centuries of the Church, make any difference in this regard: ''Therefore the Blessed Virgin is invoked by the Church under the titles of Advocate, Auxiliatrix, Adjutrix, and Mediatrix. These, however, are to be so understood that they neither take away from nor add anything to the dignity and efficacy of Christ the one Mediator.''[11] This very balanced formulation has an advantage over the correction mentioned above, in that it helps the Church to understand better what its own healing service, in the image of Mary, is to be, and how it can exercise that service, namely, in the same loving submission to Christ and by keeping in view the life of Mary:

> The Church, moreover, contemplating Mary's mysterious sanctity, imitating her charity, and faithfully fulfilling the Father's will, becomes herself a mother by accepting God's word in faith. For by her preaching and by baptism she brings forth to a new and immortal life children who are conceived of the Holy Spirit and born of God.[12]

Here we encounter precisely the idea of the Church's duty and privilege of healing that we sketched in chapter two, "Healing Through the Sacrament of the Church." The healing proper to the Church does not consist in the relief of symptoms but in freeing people from the temporal limitations of their earthly existence through the gift of eternal life. This healing takes place through the Church, according to the motherly example of Mary, when, in the sacrament of baptism and in the personal encounter with the Word of God, the human person, who already has a bodily existence (whether as child or adult), is born to a new life, that is, to life in the Spirit, to the everlasting life of which human beings had despoiled themselves through original sin, by which they cut themselves off from God.

Unity with the Communion of Saints

That the real healing of human persons means the removal of the temporal limitations of their earthly existence, and their salvation to eternal life, is a very basic insight for every Christian because it helps us to a better understanding of the indissoluble unity of the Church in heaven and the Church on earth. In the seventh chapter of the Constitution on the Church, which concerns the communion of saints, the Council emphasizes the unity between the pilgrims here on earth and those who have gone to the Father in the peace of Christ: "For by reason of the fact that those in heaven are more closely united with Christ, they establish the whole Church more firmly in holiness, lend nobility to the worship which the Church offers on earth to God, and in many ways contribute to its greater upbuilding (cf. 1 Cor 12:12-27)."[13] The concrete meaning of this is decisive for our daily lives: without the constant and intensive cooperation of those who already belong to the "Church in heaven," the efforts of the "Church on earth" are in danger of dissipating themselves in sociological and psychological activities. In that case, of course, a lot goes on in the Church, often with a great deal of engagement and even with much personal sacrifice—but nobody is healed and saved by it. There is much production, but little fruit. We proclaim all sorts of things, but not the reign of *God*.

Without the constant aid of Mary and the communion of saints, our proclamation remains ideology and our pastoral care is only a set of suggestions. And in both of those, the new sects and youth religions are ahead of us.

To put the matter more plainly, when I find that I as a Christian am unpersuasive, helpless, and lacking in success, it serves me right because it is usually my own fault: I have not taken advantage of the authority given me by Christ and have not trusted in the advocacy of Mary and the saints. I may want to heal and save other people—but without the Holy Spirit. That cannot "work": it can have no healing function.

The binding reality between God and humanity, between the Church in heaven and the Church on earth, is and remains the Holy Spirit. Otherwise there is no life in the Spirit; without the Spirit nothing can be sound and whole. Only through the Spirit can the Pentecost event, the outpouring of God's Spirit on all flesh, become the constant and yet ever-new reality of our daily lives, in which "we live and move and have our being" (Acts 17:28) and through which we ourselves and others are healed and sanctified, that is, delivered from all the fears and compulsions of this world to the only real freedom: the freedom of the children of God.

In the step-by-step development of this freedom we are,

of course, still in midcourse, but nevertheless striving toward fulfillment:

> Joined with Christ in the Church and signed with the Holy Spirit "who is the pledge of our inheritance" (Eph 1:14), we are truly called [children] of God and such we are (cf. 1 John 3:1). But we have not yet appeared with Christ in the state of glory (cf. Col 3:4), in which we shall be like to God, since we shall see Him as He is (cf. 1 John 3:2).[14]

Even though it is clear from this text that our perfection is not yet, and that we will be fully healed and liberated only when we encounter the Savior face to face, it shows just as plainly what the orientation of our whole Christian existence, both our proclamation and our pastoral work, including our service to the sick, must be: the glory of God and our share in that glory, from which come all salvation and all healing.

On this journey, which occupies our whole being, Mary and the communion of saints can be living guides for us—especially because they, in their poverty and humility, never wish to be the final objects of our devotion, but always point to the one real goal: "for by its very nature every genuine testimony of love which we show to those in heaven tends toward and terminates in Christ, who is the crown of all saints. Through him it tends toward and terminates in God, who is wonderful in His saints and is magnified in them."[15] The text also says of this important mediating and unifying role of the saints: ". . . our companionship with the saints joins us to Christ, from whom as from their fountain and head issue every grace and the life of God's People itself."[16]

The Role of Liturgy and Sacraments

In being living guides for us to Christ, Mary and the saints also make the sacraments accessible to us as a very personal, though also mysterious, encounter with Christ within his Church. In many prefaces we pray with the priest in the Eucharistic celebration: "Now, with angels and archangels, and the whole company of heaven, we sing the unending hymn of your praise: Holy, holy, holy.'' This sentence can act as a turning point for our entire Christian life: together with the Church in heaven and on earth we acknowledge God's holiness, God's heavenly glory, and the divine advent in this world as the least among us of the One who gives his life out of love for his friends—that life that he received from the Father as an undeserved gift and hands on to us: ''through his wounds we are healed.''

The Council expressly emphasizes again the role of the liturgy and of the sacraments in this unifying of heaven and earth for our sanctification and healing: ''Our union with the Church in heaven is put into effect in its noblest manner when with common rejoicing we celebrate together the praise of the divine Majesty. . . . Such is especially the case in the sacred liturgy, where the power of the Holy Spirit acts upon us through sacramental signs.''[17] Here it is plain that the praise of God in the celebration of the liturgy and the sacraments is anything but a luxury that remains in some sense optional, left to our mood and pleasure. The praise of God in the community of the Church reveals itself as the most effective means for our healing and sanctification, for it gives us the most intensive share in the glory of God, and that is true in the highest degree of the celebration of the sacraments.

Notes

1. *LG* 1.

2. *Ibid.*, 55.

3. *Ibid.*, 56.

4. *Adv. haer.* III, 22, 4, quoted in *LG* 56.

5. *Epist.* 22, 21, quoted in *LG* 56.

6. *LG* 58.

7. *Ibid.*

8. *Ibid.*, 61.

9. *Ibid.*, 60.

10. *Ibid.*

11. *Ibid.*, 62.

12. *Ibid.*, 64.

13. *Ibid.*, 49.

14. *Ibid.*, 48.

15. *Ibid.*, 50.

16. *Ibid.*

17. *Ibid.*